Risk Management in Portfolios, Programs, and Projects: A Practice Guide

Risk Management in Portfolios, Programs, and Projects: A Practice Guide (paperback)

Library of Congress Cataloging-in-Publication Data has been applied for.

ISBN: 978-1-62825-816-5

Published by: Project Management Institute, Inc.
                       18 Campus Blvd., Ste. 150
                       Newtown Square, Pennsylvania 19073-3299 USA
                       PMI.org
                       Phone: +1 610 356 4600
                       Email: customercare@pmi.org

To place an order or for pricing information, please contact Independent Publishers Group:

            Independent Publishers Group
            Order Department
            814 North Franklin Street
            Chicago, IL 60610 USA
            Phone: 800 888 4741
            Fax: +1 312 337 5985
            Email: orders@ipgbook.com (For orders only)

Notice

The Project Management Institute, Inc. (PMI) standards and guideline publications, of which the document contained herein is one, are developed through a voluntary consensus standards development process. This process brings together volunteers and/or seeks out the views of persons who have an interest in the topic covered by this publication. While PMI administers the process and establishes rules to promote fairness in the development of consensus, it does not write the document and it does not independently test, evaluate, or verify the accuracy or completeness of any information or the soundness of any judgments contained in its standards and guideline publications.

PMI disclaims liability for any personal injury, property or other damages of any nature whatsoever, whether special, indirect, consequential or compensatory, directly or indirectly resulting from the publication, use of application, or reliance on this document. PMI disclaims and makes no guaranty or warranty, expressed or implied, as to the accuracy or completeness of any information published herein, and disclaims and makes no warranty that the information in this document will fulfill any of your particular purposes or needs. PMI does not undertake to guarantee the performance of any individual manufacturer or seller's products or services by virtue of this standard or guide.

In publishing and making this document available, PMI is not undertaking to render professional or other services for or on behalf of any person or entity, nor is PMI undertaking to perform any duty owed by any person or entity to someone else. Anyone using this document should rely on his or her own independent judgment or, as appropriate, seek the advice of a competent professional in determining the exercise of reasonable care in any given circumstances. Information and other standards on the topic covered by this publication may be available from other sources, which the user may wish to consult for additional views or information not covered by this publication.

PMI has no power, nor does it undertake to police or enforce compliance with the contents of this document. PMI does not certify, test, or inspect products, designs, or installations for safety or health purposes. Any certification or other statement of compliance with any health or safety-related information in this document shall not be attributable to PMI and is solely the responsibility of the certifier or maker of the statement.

Preface

Risk Management in Portfolios, Programs, and Projects: A Practice Guide is a supplemental resource aligned with the PMI series of American National Standards Institute (ANSI)-approved standards, bringing consistency to the customer experience across the PMI publications portfolio. Organizations must adapt their visions, missions, and objectives to changing environments; therefore, PMI practice guides are evolving with them. In addition, the goal of *A Guide to the Project Management Body of Knowledge (PMBOK® Guide)* is to adapt and implement new project management perspectives and the approaches used to increase benefits and generate value for organizations.

This presents a new opportunity to align *Risk Management in Portfolios, Programs, and Projects: A Practice Guide* with those shifting perspectives related to risk management. During the last few years in particular, new trends have emerged; new management skills are requested in the market; and people continue to improve their capabilities, increasing their knowledge and developing abilities to contribute to the objectives of their organizations.

The *PMBOK® Guide*—Seventh Edition made several changes in the structure and content of the guide, with an enhanced focus on delivering value to organizations and their stakeholders. Those changes were incorporated in the new *Risk Management in Portfolios, Programs, and Projects: A Practice Guide*, changing the Knowledge Areas to the eight project management performance domains, aligning the concept of a system for value delivery, implementing agile approaches in the risk management process, and including a case study to make the content more relatable to project managers.

The new *Risk Management in Portfolios, Programs, and Projects: A Practice Guide* also aligns risk management more closely with the updated PMI Talent Triangle®, integrating the required skills in Ways of Working, Business Acumen, and Power Skills. These new ways of working will help project professionals navigate business changes and connect outcomes to generating greater value for organizations. Part of the objective of *Risk Management in Portfolios, Programs, and Projects: A Practice Guide* is to identify the risk management skills that organizations need to increase project success and value.

The previous edition of *The Standard for Risk Management in Portfolios, Programs, and Projects* focused on processes, tools, and techniques, and was aligned with the Process Groups and Knowledge Areas. *Risk Management in Portfolios, Programs, and Projects: A Practice Guide* responds to the elements that stakeholders have requested in their feedback: It improves the usefulness of the techniques, tools, processes, and good practices of risk management; aligns risk management practices with performance domains and portfolio, program, and project management principles; and is focused on realizing benefits and value through project outputs and outcomes.

Table of Contents

List of Figures and Tables

Figures

Tables

Introduction

Risk is an uncertain event or condition that, if it occurs, has a positive or negative effect on one or more project objectives. Positive risks are opportunities, while negative risks are threats.

The practice of risk management includes developing a strategy for identifying, analyzing, and prioritizing risks; planning and implementing appropriate responses; and monitoring risks on an ongoing basis until the portfolio, program, or project is completed. Identified risks may or may not materialize, but it is important to monitor them as they can have a significant impact on a portfolio, program, project, or operations. Consequently, risk management is an essential aspect of the business environment and organizational activities. This practice guide describes the application of risk management within an enterprise risk management (ERM) context that includes the portfolio, program, and project levels. Ultimately, risk management shapes the decision-making processes across the organization and within each of its components.

Risk management is essential for portfolios, programs, and projects to be successful; to be delivered on time with quality; and to fully realize the benefits and value these components bring to their organizations. A vital technical and managerial skill, risk management is also augmented by "soft" or "interpersonal" skills that foster collaboration with others and empower project professionals to succeed in the workplace. Furthermore, this dynamic range of abilities, also known as "power skills," significantly enhances the performance of multiple key drivers of success, including benefits realization management (BRM) maturity, organization agility, and project management maturity, according to the *PMI Pulse of the Profession®—Power Skills: Redefining Project Success* report [1].[1]

Risk management allows an organization to:

- Anticipate and manage change;

- Cultivate a corporate culture that balances risk, creativity, innovation, safety, and thoughtfulness;

- Be more agile and adaptable to lean innovation and startups, while also supporting organizational agility and resilience;

- Improve decision-making process;

- Proactively implement potentially lower-cost/time preventive actions instead of higher-cost/time corrective actions to issues;

- Engage stakeholders effectively;

- Increase the chances to realize opportunities for the benefit of the organization;

- Integrate sustainable, continuous improvement throughout the life cycle of the portfolio, program, or project;

- Promote awareness of uncertainties and associated impacts; and

- Act upon the transformations taking place in the organizational environment.

Risk management also establishes interconnected relationships among portfolios, programs, and projects—working with different approaches and frameworks such as adaptive, predictive, or hybrid—and links these connections to ERM and organizational strategy, with a focus on value

---

[1] The numbers in brackets refer to the list of references at the end of this practice guide.

delivery. As a result, this practice guide is useful and applicable to any organization, regardless of industry, location, size, or approach.

1.1 Purpose of This Practice Guide

This practice guide describes the concepts and definitions associated with risk management and highlights the essential components of risk management for integration into the various management and governance layers of portfolios, programs, and projects—with the following major objectives:

- Describe the fundamentals of risk management,

- Support the objectives of ERM and demonstrate how activities link to ERM, and

- Apply risk management principles, as appropriate, to portfolio, program, and project management performance domains as described in PMI standards.

This practice guide fulfills an organizational need to provide good practices for risk management in portfolio, program, and project management that defines the essential considerations for risk management practitioners. It expands upon the existing knowledge contained within the relevant sections of PMI standards.

This practice guide can be used to harmonize practices among ERM and portfolio, program, and project management, regardless of the life cycle approach taken for delivering value to the organization's strategy. In addition, organizations are increasingly requiring practitioners to use risk management practices in portfolio, program, and project management as integral parts of their ERM framework.

1.2 Approach of This Practice Guide

This practice guide presents the *why, what,* and *how* of risk management and elaborates on the following concepts:

- Purpose and benefits of risk management;

- Principles and concepts of risk management in portfolios, programs, and projects;

- Risk management life cycle in portfolios, programs, and projects; and

- Integration of risk management within portfolios, programs, and projects.

This practice guide provides guidance on integrating risk management practices into all key areas of enterprise, portfolio, program, and project management. Its aim is to ensure that risk management is considered as an inherent and natural part of all management levels. This practice guide also strives to provide direction and guidance while avoiding the imposition of uniformity of processes. Furthermore, this practice guide focuses more on intended outcomes than on deliverables, thus aligning to the principles-based approach adopted for *A Guide to the Project Management Body of Knowledge (PMBOK® Guide)* [2].

When planning and implementing risk management, it is essential that each team considers the characteristics of its organization, portfolio, program, or project and tailors its risk management approach accordingly. For example, in adaptive and hybrid project environments, the need for ongoing feedback is greater because the project teams are exploring and developing project elements within specific increments. Also, the requirements for adaptive projects are not well defined at the start, so a stronger emphasis on iterative risk management is needed because of the higher level of uncertainty. The approaches and techniques presented in this practice guide are based on risk management principles that can be applied when designing specific management or business processes adapted to the organizational environment and nature of the work.

1.3 Audience for This Practice Guide

This practice guide provides guidance to stakeholders participating in a portfolio, program, or project. This includes, but is not limited to, portfolio managers, program managers, project managers, project coordinators, project practitioners, project planners, business analysts, risk managers, risk consultants, consultants, agile practitioners, agile consultants, product owners, sponsors, and vendors who:

- Work on a portfolio, program, project, or initiative either full or part time;

- Work in a portfolio, program, or project management office;

- Are responsible for identifying and/or managing the risks of an initiative (portfolio, program, or project);

- Teach or study risk management; and

- Are involved in any aspect of the project value delivery chain.

1.4 Principles of Risk Management

The seven principles outlined in Sections 1.4.1 through 1.4.7 guide the risk management process and are integral to effective risk management. They are:

- 1.4.1 Strive to Achieve Excellence in the Practice of Risk Management

- 1.4.2 Align Risk Management with Organizational Strategy, Governance Practices, and Project Management Performance Domains

- 1.4.3 Focus on the Higher Risk Value

- 1.4.4 Optimize Risk Responses to Focus on Value Realization

- 1.4.5 Foster a Culture That Embraces Risk Management

- 1.4.6 Navigate Complexity Using Risk Management to Enable Successful Outcomes and Value Realization

- 1.4.7 Continuously Improve Risk Management Competencies

1.4.1 Strive to Achieve Excellence in the Practice of Risk Management

Risk management allows organizations and teams to increase the predictability of outcomes, both qualitatively and quantitatively, and improves the delivery of value supporting the organization's strategy. This principle is about reaching the appropriate level of organizational process maturity (the ability of an organization to apply a certain set of processes in a consistent manner) and the optimal level of performance. Excellence in risk management is not achieved by the strict and exhaustive application of related processes. Rather, it can be attained by (a) balancing the benefits to be obtained with the associated cost and (b) tailoring the risk management processes to the characteristics of the organization and its portfolios, programs, and projects. Process excellence in risk management is itself a risk management strategy.

Effective and appropriate risk management can reduce individual and overall threats while increasing individual and overall opportunities in a portfolio, program, project, or operation.

1.4.2 Align Risk Management with Organizational Strategy, Governance Practices, and Project Management Performance Domains

The practice of risk management in organizations is developed and evolved in coexistence with other organizational processes such as strategy and governance. The nature of portfolios, programs, and projects is such that circumstances may change frequently. Adaptability, agility, and resiliency are critical in risk management in order to respond to changing conditions and recover quickly from a setback or failure. Adjustments become necessary as the organization evolves (e.g., when changes to decision-making processes, timing, scope, and speed are made). The varying types of adjustments to risk management practices will be informed by the ongoing evaluation of the exposure to risk whenever these changes are implemented as recommended by the project management principle of optimizing risk responses. Establishing an appropriate cadence of risk reviews and feedback sessions with stakeholders is helpful for navigating project risk and being proactive with risk responses. Risk management interacts with the Stakeholders, Team, Development Approach and Life Cycle, Planning, Project Work, Delivery, Measurement, and Uncertainty project management performance domains, so successful risk management should be built seamlessly into these activities.

1.4.3 Focus on the Higher Risk Value

Successful organizations are able to effectively and efficiently identify and respond to the risks that directly influence goals and objectives. The challenge for most organizations is making the best use of resources by focusing on the right risks. This depends on the characteristics of the organization and its environment, internal maturity, culture, and organizational strategy. Determining the most impactful risks can be difficult. Organizations iteratively develop and improve their ability by refining the processes for risk prioritization. Organizations should also strengthen their capacity to anticipate threats and opportunities; maintain an acute awareness of the environment in which their project is implemented; and constantly monitor changes in the technical, social, political, market, and economic environments, as recommended in the Uncertainty project management performance domain.

1.4.4 Optimize Risk Responses to Focus on Value Realization

Risk management seeks to find the right balance among risk exposure, the cost of managing the risk, and the expected creation or realization of business value. Risk responses should be appropriate for the significance of the risk. The risk responses should be aligned to a planned strategy to achieve the desired value. Organizations should strike a comprehensive balance among the risk exposure and the potential costs and benefits of the portfolios, programs, and projects, and then make provisions for contingency reserves and buffers, thus securing the means to effectively respond to a risk if it materializes.

1.4.5 Foster a Culture That Embraces Risk Management

Risk management is an inherent and essential part of the portfolio, program, and project management framework. The practice of risk management is propagated, recognized, and encouraged throughout the organization. A culture of risk management encourages (a) the proactive identification of threats and (b) the identification of opportunities by cultivating a positive mindset within the organization—one that is more open to accepting and harnessing the positive innovations and changes impacting the various initiatives. It is important to identify the organizational culture, the behavior of the project management team, and environmental factors to begin implementing a risk management culture across functions or areas of the organization. Risk management should be integrated as part of the project management team's culture by deliberately including it within team norms, as well as by modeling risk management practices through the behaviors and actions of project team management.

1.4.6 Navigate Complexity Using Risk Management to Enable Successful Outcomes and Value Realization

Managing risk is critical to navigating, and even reducing, complexity and uncertainty within organizational initiatives. It is not an easy task as complexity is the result of human behavior, system interactions, uncertainty, rapid changes in the environment, technological innovation, and ambiguity. Yet, the ability to identify and manage risk depends directly on the type and level of complexity within an initiative.

Take project complexity, for example, which is the culmination of a multitude of individual elements that work toward a common goal within a portfolio, program, or project. It can be effectively controlled through risk management by clarifying the objectives, requirements, and scope of a particular initiative; identifying potential risks; and creating a plan to address such risks, thus reducing the possibility of unforeseen complexities that may be hindering the initiative.

In fact, the more organizations navigate complexity using risk management, the more effectively they can optimize the use of resources, increase returns on investment, and improve overall performance and business results. A strong focus on risk management can lay the groundwork for attaining success and valuable outcomes.

1.4.7 Continuously Improve Risk Management Competencies

The nature of risks to which an organization is exposed—and the available technology to manage those risks—is changing. Technology, such as artificial intelligence (AI) and machine learning (ML), allows organizations to manage risks more effectively and better focus on their impacts. By continuously improving risk management competencies, a team can bolster its ability to anticipate threats and opportunities, understand the consequences of issues, and balance the risk, responding to any associated costs and its value realization systematically. This will allow the team to:

- Maximize the probability of positive risks. If a positive risk occurs, it may provide an opportunity that could lead to benefits, such as reduced time, costs, or effort; and

- Decrease exposure to negative risks to avoid issues, such as delays, cost overruns, loss of reputation, or any other threats that may harm the organization.

Consequently, the team can become more proficient and efficient in its risk management approach.

1.5 Structure of This Practice Guide

This practice guide can be used to review portfolio, program, and project management processes from a risk management perspective. It is organized as follows:

Section 1   Introduction

Section 2   Context and Key Concepts of Risk Management

Section 3   Framework for Risk Management in Portfolio, Program, and Project Management

Section 4   Risk Management Life Cycle in Portfolio, Program, and Project Management

Section 5   Risk Management in the Context of Portfolio Management

Section 6   Risk Management in the Context of Program Management

Section 7   Risk Management in the Context of Project Management

Appendix X1   Contributors and Reviewers of *Risk Management in Portfolios, Programs, and Projects: A Practice Guide*

Appendix X2   Techniques for the Risk Management Framework

Appendix X3   Risk Classification

Context and Key Concepts of Risk Management

Risk is inherently present in all organizations. While it presents challenges, it may also offer a competitive advantage when both threats and opportunities are managed proactively. Risk management provides a comprehensive, integrated framework for addressing and managing risk at all levels of the organization, from portfolios through programs, projects, and operations. Stakeholders should proactively identify risks throughout the portfolio, program, project, and organization to eliminate or minimize the impacts of threats as well as maximize the impact of opportunities.

In today's dynamic and interconnected world, businesses face a wide range of risks, including technological, regulatory, market, and competitive risks. Other risks could be because of increased globalization that can expose organizations to risks originating from different parts of the world, thus necessitating a more holistic, integrated approach to risk management.

Furthermore, regulatory requirements related to risk management have become more stringent, requiring organizations to implement robust risk management processes to ensure compliance and avoid penalties.

The pace of change in business environments, driven by technological advancements and changing consumer preferences, has made it more challenging for organizations to anticipate and respond to risks effectively.

2.1 Key Concepts and Definitions

All organizations face uncertainties with both internal and external events. Uncertain challenges may be dealt with by formulating and applying a sound business strategy focused on realizing a set of objectives and managing risks. Risk management provides insight into risks that need to be addressed in support of reaching those objectives, while also taking advantage of opportunities. When such opportunities occur, they are called benefits; when negative risks or threats occur, they are called issues. If the overall threats or issues to the portfolio, program, or project are too high, the organization may choose to cancel the effort.

2.1.1 Risk

An individual risk is an uncertain event or condition that, if it occurs, has a positive or negative effect on one or more objectives.

For example, a positive risk is a potential upcoming change in policy that could benefit a project. A negative risk can be an unanticipated increase of labor or material cost, which may cause the project to surpass the original budget. In this case, the problem becomes more specific, with a causal factor, instead of just stating that the project will be over budget. Overall risk is the impact of uncertainty that affects organizational objectives at different levels or aspects.

Risks can arise from all sources of uncertainty and assumptions, including individual risks at the portfolio, program, and project levels. These risks represent the exposure of the organization and its stakeholders to the consequences of uncertainty regarding the organization's strategy and business objectives. Once a risk occurs, it is then managed within the various governance layers (enterprise, portfolio, program, and project) by driving the resulting outcomes.

Uncertainty is inherent to the nature of portfolios, programs, and projects. Uncertainty refers to a lack of comprehension or awareness regarding issues, events, or potential solutions. It involves assessing probabilities of various actions, reactions, and outcomes. Uncertainty encompasses unknown-unknowns and black swans, representing emerging factors beyond current knowledge or experience.

Risk both arises out of uncertainty and generates uncertainty through a lack of awareness about potential outcomes or the likelihood of occurrence. Thus, the more risks one can identify, the better one can plan and prepare for them. Some of the key factors determining the ability to identify risks include ambiguity and uncertainty, which is a state of being unclear, of not knowing what to expect or how to comprehend a situation, or continuously evaluating the common sources of complexity, as explained in the *PMBOK® Guide* [2]. When ambiguity is low, the level of integral information is sufficient, and there is clarity and a high degree of certainty in terms of what to expect, which allows for the identification of risks. Though complexity cannot be controlled, project teams can modify their activities to control and address impacts that occur as a result of complexity, as described in the *PMBOK® Guide* [2]. When it comes to uncertainty and ambiguity, assessment and open evaluation drive risk management efforts. All initiatives, including portfolios, programs, and projects, possess risks since they are unique undertakings with varying degrees of uncertainty.

Assessments and open evaluations help determine the right risk management strategy as well as how risks will be handled across the entire portfolio, program, and project management life cycles, including their various stages and interactions. Open evaluation in risk management refers to the transparent and inclusive assessment of risks, and involves actively involving stakeholders, experts, and relevant parties in the evaluation process to gather diverse perspectives and insights.

Establishing a frequent synchronization, rhythm, cadence, or schedule of review-and-feedback sessions (e.g., weekly, biweekly, monthly, etc.) for team members and stakeholders is helpful for navigating risks and being proactive with risk management. In projects following an adaptive approach, if used by the team, a daily meeting (e.g., daily standup meetings) can be instrumental in identifying potential risks. During such meetings, potential obstacles or impediments can be identified, thus reducing the likelihood of these becoming issues.

A SWOT (strengths, weaknesses, opportunities, threats) analysis can help with risk assessment, enabling a team to identify risks in a portfolio, program, or project. SWOT analysis evaluates initiatives from each of the SWOT perspectives, identifies and lists organizational strengths and weaknesses, and then derives opportunities from both the strengths and the threats from those weaknesses. Below are examples of how this approach can be carried out.

2.1.1.1 Strengths

Strengths are characteristics that give an organization a competitive advantage over others and contribute to the success of portfolios, programs, and projects. This is accomplished by:

- Identifying portfolios, programs, or projects in trouble more easily;
- Minimizing surprises;
- Providing better-quality data for decision-making;
- Enhancing communication; and
- Improving budget estimates.

2.1.1.2 Weaknesses

Weaknesses place an organization at a disadvantage and negatively impact the success of portfolios, programs, and projects. Examples include:

- Exorbitant training costs,
- Loss of focus due to automation, and
- Data security issues.

2.1.1.3 Opportunities

Opportunities are risks that would have a positive effect on one or more project objectives. Opportunity management helps to point out and understand the possible ways in which objectives can be achieved more successfully.

Moving beyond the traditional view of risk as a value destroyer to seeing it as a potential value enhancer requires creativity and vision, and may help organizations to develop a system for allowing these opportunities to flourish and result in organizational success.

A consistent portfolio, program, and project management system helps to:

- Identify and assess opportunities that are often linked, and
- Improve the organization's ability to accept and pursue opportunities.

Risk responses should be developed for the opportunities and should be reviewed to see whether the planned responses may have introduced any secondary risks.

2.1.1.4 Threats

Threats are risks that would have a negative effect on one or more project objectives. Threat management specifically focuses on addressing potential negative events or threats, and is a subset of risk management. It involves the use of risk management resources to:

- Describe risks;
- Analyze risk attributes (e.g., specific characteristics or qualities associated with risks);
- Evaluate the probability of risk occurrence and impacts, as well as other characteristics; and
- Implement a planned response, when appropriate.

A response to a specific threat may include multiple strategies. If the threat cannot be avoided, it may be mitigated to a level where it becomes viable to transfer or to accept it and respond in such a way that the project is not negatively affected. Creating a contingency reserve will support the risk response strategies by ensuring sufficient funds are set aside in the event of a risk being identified or other applicable events (e.g., supply chain issues or budget overruns).

Similar to managing opportunities, handling threats is a staged process. Both use a structured life cycle framework to ensure the process is robust and complete, as described in Section 4. Should threats occur, they are called issues and are listed in the issue log.

2.1.2 Risk Attitude

Risk attitude is a disposition toward uncertainty, adopted explicitly or implicitly by individuals and groups, driven by perception and previous personal experience, and evidenced by observable behavior. Risk attitude represents an organization's approach to assessing and eventually pursuing, retaining, taking, or turning away from risk. It is a function of risk appetite and risk threshold and can range from risk averse to risk seeking.

Organizations seek to establish a consistent method for evaluating and responding to risk across the enterprise. One obstacle to developing that consistency is an individual's different or inconsistent attitudes toward risks—and those attitudes may vary according to the circumstance.

However, organizations can choose to change the risk attitudes of individuals and groups by providing them with tools and techniques they can use to learn how to assess each situation and then consciously choose a risk attitude explicitly. This empowers them to select the attitude most appropriate to the situation and offers the best chance of achieving portfolio, program, and project objectives.

In summary, risk attitude is an individual or group preference when evaluating a risk situation in a favorable or unfavorable way and then acting accordingly. While risk attitudes are not necessarily stable or homogeneous, organizations can adopt tools and techniques designed to coach and mentor staff on how to change their risk attitudes. It is important to identify and assess the level of adaptability and resiliency of the organization. Adaptability is the ability to respond to changing conditions, and resiliency is the ability to absorb impacts and recover quickly from a setback or failure. The risk attitude will reflect the level of adaptability and resiliency of the team.

2.1.3 Risk Appetite

Risk appetite is how much uncertainty an organization is okay with while pursuing its goals. It's about finding a middle ground between being open to taking risks and being cautious. Other elements that complement the appetite for risk include risk tolerance and risk capacity.

A risk appetite determination represents the start of embracing risk. Figure 2-1 shows the interrelationship of risk appetite and its direct influence on business strategy, the risk management framework, and the underlying organizational policies and processes. The resulting risk appetite determination defines the amount and type of risk that the organization is willing to accept in order to meet its strategic objectives.

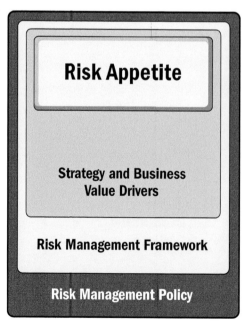

Figure 2-1. Risk Appetite and Its Relationship with Organizational Strategy

Additionally, risk appetite expresses the level of risk the organization is willing to take in pursuit of its portfolio, program, and project objectives. Portfolio, program, and project risk is a multifaceted rather than singular concept.

As organizations grow, expand, and evolve, so do the risks they face. The type, prominence, and appetite for risks may change at different points in the life cycle of an organization and during the life cycle of its portfolios, programs, and projects.

The risk appetite of an organization should take into consideration some of the more common sources of complexity, such as:

- **Human behavior.** The interplay of conduct, demeanors, attitudes, and experiences of people that influence risk attitude and risk appetite.

- **System behavior.** The result of dynamic interdependencies within and among project elements.

- **Uncertainty and ambiguity.** A state of being unclear, of not knowing what to expect or how to comprehend a situation.

- **Technological innovation.** New technology, along with the uncertainty of how that technology will be used, contributes to complexity.

These sources of complexity could impact the risk appetite of an organization, project team, or individual person. It is important to take into consideration these common sources of complexity to understand the variance of risk appetites among organizations, project teams, or individual persons.

2.1.4 Risk Threshold

Risk threshold is the measure of acceptable variation around an objective that reflects the risk appetite of the organization and its stakeholders. A key element of risk strategy is the establishment and monitoring of enterprise, portfolio, program, and project risk thresholds. Risk threshold thus represents the level of risk below which an organization will accept, and above which an organization will not accept.

Examples of risk thresholds include:

- Minimum level of risk exposure for a risk to be included in the risk register,

- Qualitative or quantitative definitions of risk rating, and

- Maximum level of risk exposure that can be managed before an escalation is triggered.

A project manager conducts a qualitative analysis of identified risks, prioritizes them based on their probability of occurrence and impact, and establishes risk response plans. Consider a software development project aiming to create a new mobile application. In qualitative risk analysis, the project team and stakeholders identify potential risks related to the project's objectives, timeline, resources, and technology. Some identified risks could include integrating new technologies or platforms that the team is not familiar with, which could lead to delays or errors in development.

For data to be suitable for quantitative risk analysis, it should be studied for a long period of time or observed in multiple situations.

Establishing risk thresholds is an integral step in linking portfolio, program, and project risk management to strategy alignment. This is performed as part of the definition of risk policies in the organization or, if common definitions do not exist, as part of the project definition before including it in the portfolio. Based on the risk appetite of the organization, governance may also be responsible for ensuring risk thresholds are established and observed, and for deciding when a risk should be escalated to a higher governance level. Making use of technological advances and emergent technologies such as artificial intelligence, organizations can automate the determination of when risk thresholds are reached and put in place predetermined workflows that include escalation to higher governance levels when risk thresholds are exceeded.

The risk threshold reflects the risk appetite. Therefore, a risk threshold of ±5% around a cost objective reflects a lower risk appetite than a risk threshold of ±10%. The risk appetite and risk threshold inform how the project team and other stakeholders navigate risk in a project.

2.1.5 Uncertainty

Uncertainty is directly related to risk and it stems from a lack of understanding and awareness of issues, events, paths to follow, or solutions to pursue. Broadly, it refers to a state of not knowing or unpredictability. According to the *PMBOK® Guide* [2], successful navigation of uncertainty starts with an understanding of the larger environment in which the organization operates. Options for responding to uncertainty may include:

- Gathering more information,

- Preparing for multiple outcomes,

- Set-based design, and

- Building in resilience.

2.2 Risk Management in Organizations

The organization's governance body is ultimately responsible for setting, confirming, and enforcing risk appetite and risk management principles as part of its governance oversight. An organization's governance also determines which risk management processes are appropriate in terms of organizational strategy, scope, context, and content.

The enterprise risk function often resides in the executive management organization due to the direct relationship between the success of achieving organizational strategic goals and employing an effective risk management process.

When assessing the seriousness of a risk or combination of risks, uncertainty and its effect on endeavors or objectives are considered. The uncertainty dimension is commonly described as *probability* and the effect is often referred to as *impact*.

The definition of risk includes both (a) distinct events that are uncertain but can be clearly described and (b) more general conditions that are less specific but may also give rise to uncertainty.

The definition of risk also encompasses uncertain events that could have a negative or positive effect on objectives. Both of these uncertain situations are considered to be risks when they could have an adverse or positive effect on the achievement of objectives. It is essential to address both situations within an enterprise, portfolio, program, or project risk management process.

Addressing threats and opportunities together (i.e., addressing both in the same analysis and coordinating the responses to both when they overlap) allows for synergies and efficiencies.

It is important to distinguish risks from risk-related features. *Causes* are events or circumstances that currently exist or are certain to exist in the future, which may give rise to risks. *Effects* are conditional future events or conditions that directly affect one or more objectives if the associated risk occurs.

A risk may have one or more causes and, if it occurs, may have one or more effects. When a risk event happens, the risk ceases to be uncertain. Threats that occur are termed *issues*, and opportunities that occur are *benefits* to the enterprise, portfolio, program, or project. Portfolio, program, and project managers are responsible for resolving these issues and managing them efficiently and effectively. Issues may entail actions that are outside the scope of the portfolio, program, and project risk management processes, or above the ability of a certain manager; therefore, these issues are escalated to a higher management level according to the organization's governance policy.

2.3 Risk Management at Different Organizational Levels

Risk management is an integrated framework that spans organizational levels. Aside from simply predicting what could happen, the aim of risk management is to develop the means to support the achievement of organizational objectives, realization of the strategic vision, and creation of value.

Risk management strongly influences decision-making at the enterprise, portfolio, program, project, and product levels. Product management considerations are applicable to projects where the deliverables are products; these fall outside of the scope of this document. At the enterprise level, the entire organizational strategy is the set of strategic and business management actions for countering business threats and exploiting business opportunities. These decisions and actions are often executed within the portfolio as part of its individual components.

The various perceptions and perspectives regarding risk management at the portfolio, program, and project management levels feed into one another in an iterative, interactive, and dynamic manner. Risks may be interconnected, have dependencies, and interact via feedback loops (see Figure 2-2). Details of these interactions are provided in Sections 5, 6, and 7.

2.3.1 Enterprise

The primary purpose of risk management is the creation and protection of value. Enterprise risk management (ERM) is an approach for identifying major risks that confront an organization as well as forecasting the significance of those risks to business processes. The way in which risks are managed reflects the organization's culture, capability, and strategy to create and sustain value. ERM addresses risks at the organizational level, including the aggregation of all risks associated with the enterprise's portfolio of programs and projects.

When exploring alternative strategies, ERM enables the alignment of each portfolio, program, and project component with the organizational strategy. ERM establishes the connections among the various governance levels through the bottom-up escalation of identified risks and the top-down definition of risk management strategies. The top-down process triggers the creation of programs, projects, and other activities aimed at exploiting specific opportunities and addressing business threats.

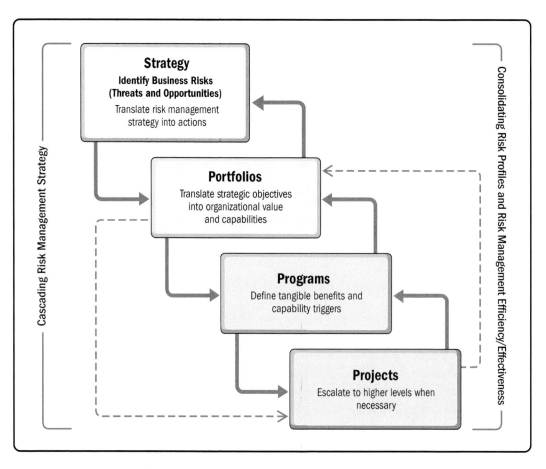

Figure 2-2. Cascading of Risk Management Strategy into Portfolios, Programs, and Projects

ERM provides a systematic, organized, and structured method for:

- Identifying and assessing the key risks an organization faces,

- Developing suitable responses,

- Communicating status with stakeholders, and

- Assigning responsibility for monitoring and managing risks in alignment with the strategic objectives of the organization.

ERM is an ongoing process that supports the plan-do-check-act (PDCA) cycle for continuous improvement. ERM is not limited to compliance and disclosure requirements, nor is it a replacement for internal controls and audits. The application of ERM varies depending on the organization and could change from year to year based on overall risk appetite, stakeholder expectations and requirements, and the internal and external environment.

There is no one-size-fits-all approach to performing ERM. Its function, structure, and activities vary with each organization. ERM ensures that all key organizational risks are addressed and properly managed and monitored, and that a culture of effective risk management is established and cascaded down to the portfolio, program, and project levels.

Risk management in the enterprise management context of integrated portfolio, program, and project management consists of:

- Elaborating the risk governance framework;

- Identifying operational and contextual risks at each level of the integrated governance framework, including both negative risks (threats) and positive risks (opportunities);

- Analyzing the identified risks from both the qualitative and quantitative perspectives and identifying the governance layer best suited to manage them, according to the escalation rules in place within the portfolio, program, and project management framework;

- Defining an appropriate risk management strategy based on increasing the probability and/or impact of positive risks (opportunities) and decreasing the probability and/or impact of negative risks (threats);

- Identifying the risk owner and assigning the risk;

- Implementing the corresponding strategies and activities related to anticipatory and/or responsive actions;

- Monitoring the effectiveness and efficiency of the risk management strategies deployed within the enterprise, portfolio, program, and project management framework;

- Ensuring alignment among portfolio, program, and project management risk governance models and the ERM strategy; and

- Promoting effective risk management within the entire enterprise through a risk management culture.

2.3.2 Portfolio

Portfolio risk management categorizes risks as structural, component, and overall risks. Structural risks are associated with the composition of a group of projects and the potential interdependencies among components. Component risks at the portfolio level are those the component manager escalates to the portfolio level for information or action. Overall, portfolio risk considers the interdependencies among components and is therefore more than just the sum of individual component risks. Risk efficiency is a key element of managing risk at the portfolio level. Risk efficiency is achieved by adjusting the mix of portfolio components to balance risk and reward so that overall portfolio risk exposure is managed.

Planning, designing, and implementing an effective portfolio risk management system depends on organizational culture, top management commitment, stakeholder engagement, and open and fair communication processes. Portfolio risk management is important for the success of managing portfolios where the value lost due to component failure is significant, or when the risks of one component impact the risks in another component. One of the purposes of portfolio risk management is to meet the strategic plan and achieve organizational goals and objectives.

As defined in *The Standard for Portfolio Management* [3], portfolio risk management ensures that components achieve the best possible success based on the organizational strategy and business model. Portfolio risk management can be viewed as the management activities related to adapting the mix of portfolio components to the evolution of the organization's business environment. Similar to enterprise strategy, the result of portfolio risk management strategy is defining and launching new components or closing other ones. Portfolio components can be responses to identified threats or opportunities in alignment with the organization's overall business strategy.

Portfolio risk management involves the identification and balancing of risk factors (environmental, human, legislation, compliance, etc.) to effectively and efficiently enable portfolio value delivery. A risk factor refers to any variable, condition, or circumstance that increases the likelihood of a negative event occurring or the severity of its impact. In various contexts, risk factors are elements that contribute to uncertainty, a potential threat, or an opportunity.

Managing risk at all levels is an active process involving continuous planning, analysis, response, and monitoring and control. A desired outcome from portfolio risk management is utilizing a structured risk-planning-and-response effort in order to reduce management inaction and decision delay. Risk not addressed at the portfolio level could be addressed through governance processes at the strategic level. In the final analysis, if a risk becomes an issue, it may be handled through the organization's portfolio, program, and project structure and not at the strategic governance level.

Risk management plays a significant role in decision-making processes—and has the capability to affect decision-making timeframes and activities. For example, identifying potential risks can lead the team to consider factors they might have otherwise overlooked, which can influence the timeframe and activities involved. It can also prompt the team to adjust their timelines or activities to respond (i.e., mitigate or avoid certain risks altogether). In addition, risk management doesn't stop once a decision is made. It involves ongoing monitoring and review of risks to ensure that the decision remains viable.

Risk management involves a comprehensive process of identifying, assessing, prioritizing, and responding to risks, including escalation to higher levels of management (i.e., program and portfolio levels) as necessary. In many cases, decisions regarding resource allocation, project prioritization, and strategic planning are informed by risk assessments and considerations.

2.3.3 Program

Program risk management strategy ensures effective management of any risk that can cause misalignment between the program roadmap and its supported objectives to organizational strategy. It includes defining program risk thresholds, performing the initial program risk assessment, and developing a program risk response strategy.

Program risk management determines how risks are to be communicated to governance layers and strategic levels of the organization. This level of strategic alignment requires that program risk thresholds take into account the organizational strategy and risk attitude. Program risks go beyond the sum of the risks from each project within the program. Program risk management applies the concepts of portfolio risk management to the set of program components.

The Standard for Program Management [4] describes program risk management strategy as:

- Identifying program risk thresholds,

- Performing an initial program risk assessment,

- Developing a high-level program risk response strategy, and

- Determining how risks are to be communicated and managed as part of governance.

Program risk management aggregates operational risks for component projects and activities and handles the specific risks at the program level, which is dependent on the layers of accountability defined in the portfolio, program, and project governance models. Also, the perspective on risk at the program level is, in many cases, more focused on the immediate impact of threats than on the expected benefit of achieving opportunities.

A program risk is an event or series of events or conditions that may affect the success of the program. These risks arise from the program components and their interactions with one another; from technical complexity, schedule, or cost constraints; and from the broader environment in which the program is managed. Two aspects of risk should be assessed during program definition: (a) an identification of the key risks that the program may encounter and (b) an assessment of the organization's willingness to accept and deal with risks, sometimes referred to as its risk appetite.

2.3.4 Project

Project risk management is addressed in the Uncertainty project management performance domain that comprises activities and functions associated with risk and uncertainty that could impact cost, schedule, or scope baselines.

The *PMBOK® Guide* [2] embeds project risk management as part of the system for value delivery for an organization by including it as one of the principles of project management—Optimize Risk Responses—and as a project management performance domain—Uncertainty. This ensures that project risk management is part of the value chain that links those and other business capabilities to advancing organizational strategy, value, and business objectives.

Risk management steps include the processes of conducting risk management planning, identification, analysis, response planning, response implementation, and monitoring risks of a project. The objectives of project risk management are to increase the probability and/or impact of opportunities and decrease those of threats, in order to increase the chances of project success. The *PMBOK® Guide* [2] states that when unmanaged, these risks have the potential to cause the project to deviate from the plan and fail to achieve the defined project objectives. Consequently, project success is directly related to the effectiveness of project risk management.

Project risk management supports project objectives by adapting or implementing the courses of action and project activities to take advantage of emerging changes in the project environment. Thus, the project baselines (e.g., scope, schedule, and cost) are risk informed. All identified risks undergo qualitative analysis, and some risks undergo quantitative analysis when the risk impacts the baseline and/or when analysis of the combined effect of multiple risks is required.

The *PMBOK® Guide* [2] states that team members should evaluate exposure to risks, both opportunities and threats, on an ongoing basis to maximize positive impacts and minimize negative impacts to the project and its outcomes. The risk responses should be appropriate for the significance of the risk, effective and realistic within the project context, agreed upon by stakeholders, and owned by an accountable person.

2.4 Key Success Factors

Enterprise (which includes organizational project management), portfolio, program, and project risk management are conducted in a manner consistent with practices and policies. In addition, portfolio, program, and project risk management are performed in a way that is appropriate to the characteristics of the endeavor. Specific criteria for the success of each risk management process are listed in the sections dealing with those processes. The key success factors for risk management that enable the realization of the principles are illustrated in Figure 2-3.

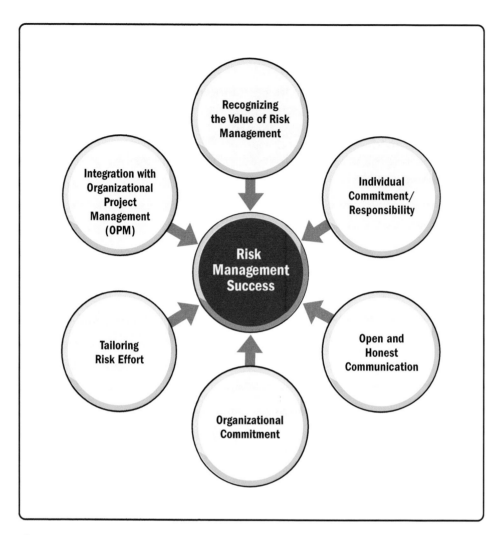

Figure 2-3. Key Success Factors for Risk Management

The key success factors include:

- **Recognizing the value of risk management.** Portfolio, program, and project risk management are recognized by organizational management, stakeholders, and team members as valuable disciplines providing a positive return on investment.

- **Individual commitment/responsibility.** Portfolio, program, and project participants and stakeholders accept responsibility for undertaking risk-related activities as required. Risk management is everyone's responsibility.

- **Open and honest communication.** Everyone is involved in the risk management process. Any actions or attitudes that hinder communication about risk reduce the effectiveness of risk management regarding proactive approaches and effective decision-making. It is important for project members to hone their power skills, such as collaborative leadership, communication, an innovative mindset, for-purpose orientation, and empathy, to ensure they can have open and honest communication with one another and their stakeholders.

- **Organizational commitment.** Organizational commitment is established only when risk management is aligned with the organization's goals, values, and ERM policies. Risk management actions may require the approval of, or response from, others at levels above the portfolio, program, or project manager.

- **Tailoring risk effort.** Risk management activities are consistent with the value of the endeavor to the organization and with its levels of risk, complexity, scale, and other organizational constraints (e.g., insufficient information, equipment interruptions, or inadequate help from other people).

- **Integration with organizational project management.** Risk management does not exist in a vacuum isolated from other organizational project management processes. Successful risk management requires the appropriate execution of organizational project management and ERM processes, including the allocation of resources necessary for the effective application of risk management.

Framework for Risk Management in Portfolio, Program, and Project Management

Risks are present in every organizational activity, especially across endeavors such as portfolios, programs, and projects. Organizational inertia is inherently risky because products and services become stale over time and organizations may lose their competitiveness due to societal and technological changes. Risks can be difficult to manage because even one can have different impacts on various components of portfolios and programs and across the various levels of an organization. Thus, risks should be handled through the organization's portfolio, program, and project structures.

Organizations and professionals need to balance threats and opportunities and the dilemma of inaction versus action. This section addresses this dilemma by providing the framework for risk management across the enterprise and its portfolio, program, and project management activities. An effective framework for risk management should cover the areas of risk identification, analysis, measurement, response, reporting and monitoring, and governance. Ideally, this framework should be flexible enough to be tailored to any organization's portfolio, program, and project context, thus ensuring positive outcomes consistently.

3.1 Business Context of Risk Management in Portfolio, Program, and Project Management

All organizations encounter internal and external factors that influence their ability to achieve desired objectives, because all organizational activities involve uncertainty and risks.

An organization manages risk through people, processes, technology, and information. Portfolio, program, and project managers are responsible for risks associated with their endeavors. These managers should work with stakeholders at various levels of the organization; apply a systematic, integrated approach to risk management; and ensure that the portfolio, programs, projects, products, and operations work together to create value for the organization. Policies, procedures, approaches, frameworks, and the governance structure, among other factors, should be taken into consideration as part of risk management.

Figure 3-1 represents the context of organizational activities, from the abstract (the top of an organization) to the specific (the bottom), where discrete tasks are completed. Risk permeates throughout the pyramid. For greater context, see how Figure 3-1 illustrates how the organizational strategy sets the direction for the vision and mission, and defines specific objectives for the organization. This is all-encompassing and includes operational and change activities.

Goals and objectives are aligned with strategies. The attainment of business benefits and value requires the execution of operational and change management plans. Organizations realize the benefits of change by executing plans and their associated activities, which result in the successful attainment of portfolio, program, and project objectives. Change by its very nature can cause uncertainty. For most organizations, change is inevitable and necessary to maintain and sustain competitiveness. To manage change successfully, organizations require a robust, well-considered strategic execution plan to implement portfolios, programs, and projects in a consistent manner over time (see Figure 3-2). This requires the adoption of an effective organizational project management implementation.

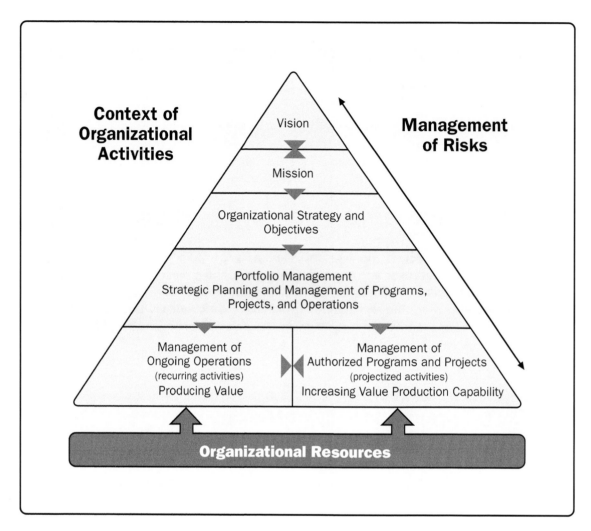

Figure 3-1. Risk across the Various Levels of the Organization

Organizational project management is a framework in which portfolio, program, and project management are aligned with strategy and integrated with organizational enablers to achieve strategic objectives. Portfolio, program, and project management target business objectives that support the organizational strategy. Linking portfolio management to strategy balances the use of resources to maximize the value delivered in executing programs, projects, and operational activities, as described in *The Standard for Portfolio Management* [3]. Some threats arise when strategy or business objectives are not aligned with the organization's mission, vision, and core values. Additional threats arise when business models and objectives do not support strategy or when endeavors, such as portfolios, programs, and projects, are not aligned with the business models and objectives. Opportunities could be enhanced when strategy and business models and objectives are well aligned. The strategy and business models and objectives should be evaluated constantly because the cadence of project deliverables could impact the program and portfolio.

3.1.1 Organizational Framework

As shown in Figure 3-3, risk management is applicable to all levels of the organization: enterprise, portfolios, programs, and projects. As discussed in previous sections of this practice guide,

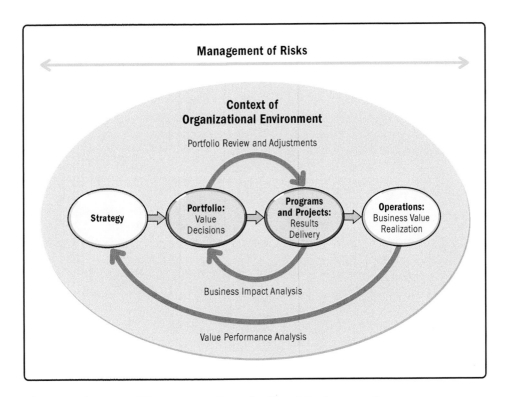

Figure 3-2. Impact of Strategy on Organizational Environment

enterprise risk management (ERM) is an approach to identifying and managing risk that reflects the organization's culture, capability, and strategy to create and sustain value. ERM covers the policies, processes, and methods by which organizations manage risks (both threats and opportunities) to advance the mission and vision of the organization and create value. Portfolio risk management derives its policies, processes, methods, and risk thresholds from the ERM framework and tailors it for the management of portfolios. Similarly, programs and projects adopt their respective risk management practices from the portfolio framework.

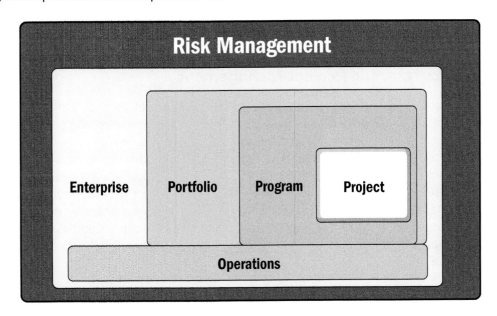

Figure 3-3. Risk Management across Levels of Organizational Activities

The governance board has a fiduciary responsibility to oversee ERM and ensure that a risk management strategy is in place. Portfolio, program, and project managers have the responsibility to implement the risk management strategy by ensuring risk management processes are in place and risk responses are optimized. These managers should also ensure risk responses are appropriate for the significance of the risk, cost effective, realistic within the project parameters, agreed upon by relevant stakeholders, and owned by a responsible person, as explained in the *PMBOK® Guide* [2]. This approach will help instill the importance and values of risk management, expected culture and behavior, and risk attitude.

3.1.2 Organizational Context

The application of ERM is influenced by industry shifts, regulations, disruptive technology, competition, business model changes, and organizational context. By understanding the context in which the organization exists, portfolio, program, and project managers can tailor the optimal approach to risk management for their endeavors and simultaneously assist the organization in assessing and responding to risks. Many factors can also impact the extent of risk management practices, including legal, economic, and behavioral factors; human health; and the effects of each decision/alternative. It is important to take into consideration the organizational culture and style (distinctive characteristics) when the portfolio, program, and project managers start evaluating these factors.

3.1.3 Strategic and Organizational Planning

Risk management in portfolios, programs, and projects aligns with setting the strategic vision, mission, goals, values, and business models and objectives of an organization, always focusing on value realization. It provides the inputs for pursuing different alternatives. Strategic goals and business models and objectives are developed to realize the organization's vision and mission in line with core values. Once these goals and objectives are set, they become inputs for risk management. If there are potential conflicts between strategic goals and the portfolio of work, then the risk is escalated to the appropriate level of management, namely ERM; portfolios, programs, and projects; or operations, as depicted in Figure 3.3.

3.1.4 Linking Planning with Execution through Portfolio, Program, and Project Management

Portfolio, program, and project management refer to different levels in the organizational project management (OPM) framework for managing capabilities and enhancing existing value or creating new value. A larger portfolio can contain subsidiary portfolios, which in themselves are component collections of programs, projects, or operations managed as groups to achieve strategic objectives. It is thus easy to see why portfolio management serves as a bridge connecting strategic planning with business execution. By focusing on selecting the right portfolio components (e.g., programs, projects, and operational initiatives), portfolio management enables organizations to achieve alignment with strategy and to invest their resources in controlling risks based on their likelihood and impact. Portfolio, program, and project management are then responsible for the implementation of risk management strategies.

These activities are performed within an environment that is full of unexpected and harmful risks. While organizational project management enables an organization to leverage its results and implementation success and supports a healthy organization within a competitive and rapidly changing environment, it is never risk free. Therefore, it is essential for organizational leaders and managers to recognize the importance of managing risks to reduce the impact of the threats and identify opportunities. This approach allows them to focus on developing an overall organizational orientation toward treating as many endeavors as appropriate and managing them individually and collectively in such a way as to support the organization's strategic goals. Portfolio, program, and project managers work inclusively to (a) identify, analyze, evaluate, prioritize, recommend, plan, and implement risk responses; (b) monitor progress; and (c) adjust risk responses as appropriate.

3.2 Scope of Accountability, Responsibility, and Authority

The accountability, responsibility, and authority of risk management are shared by key stakeholders involved in enterprise, portfolio, program, and project management. Clarity on roles and responsibilities can improve team cultures; whenever tasks are delegated to individuals or selected by project team members, it is important to clarify the scope of the following:

- *Accountability* is individual by nature and derived from a position held in the organization. Unlike responsibility, accountability cannot be shared. Accountability is related to authority in that one is usually held accountable within one's limits of authority. However, one still may be held accountable beyond one's authority to act. Furthermore, in a collaborative project team, the team will take collective ownership of the project outcomes.

- *Responsibility* resides in an individual by the assignment of a function or task. By accepting the assignment, an individual takes on the associated responsibility. The fact that others higher in the organization may also be held responsible or accountable does not diminish the responsibility held by the individual. The assigning individual is still held accountable for the delegated task, but responsibility is passed to the assigned individual.

- *Authority*, like responsibility, may be delegated and gives an individual the ability to make decisions within defined bounds. Authority denotes accountability but needs to be combined with effective leadership to motivate a group toward a common goal, influence them to align their individual interests in favor of collective effort, and achieve success as a project team rather than as individuals, as described in the *PMBOK® Guide* [2].

3.2.1 Accountability at the Enterprise Level

The objective of risk management is to apply knowledge, skills, and good practices to manage the area of focus within the risk threshold that is acceptable to the organization, whether at the enterprise, portfolio, program, or project level. The purpose is to embrace opportunities that translate to value and minimize the impact of threats to protect the organization from loss. The management of risk across the continuum of portfolios, programs, and projects requires collaboration throughout the enterprise as well as the recognition that failure to allocate the appropriate amount of resources could jeopardize the organization's strategic objectives. Effective risk management across the organization reduces threat exposure and the effects of uncertainty. An effective risk management approach will help with the accuracy of the planned allocation of risk contingency resources, increasing the project delivery reliability and the effect of project delivery execution on portfolio/program benefit realization.

Portfolio, program, and project management are responsible for supporting management policies, defining roles and responsibilities, setting targets, and overseeing implementation. The managers of the work are responsible for keeping senior management and stakeholders apprised of ongoing risk exposure and corresponding responses, thus avoiding a lack of prioritization of portfolio risks, program risks, and project risks.

3.2.2 Accountability at the Portfolio Level

Portfolios can exist for brief periods of time or as long as the organization itself. As a result, portfolio managers may oversee activities or authorize components that could take several years for the organization to recognize as valuable investments. Any change in this landscape has direct implications on the organization's strategic objectives. Specific external factors may include regulatory requirements or mandates, market conditions, supply chain disruptions, cyberattacks, geopolitical events, and environmental risks. The risk environment at the portfolio level is dynamic, complex, interdependent, and nonlinear, so change management should be implemented at the portfolio level to drive any changes and align the organization's strategic objectives.

Portfolio risk management tackles strategic, execution, and structural risks. Whereas program risk management evaluates risk across a related set of components, portfolio risk management is broad and considers risks that could impact unrelated components and operational activities within the portfolio. As a result, portfolio managers address several challenges when managing risk because portfolio-level risks encompass both external and internal factors by bridging organizational strategy to implementation. Consequently, there is a distinction among portfolio management, program management, and project management. The portfolio manager should delegate risk response measures to subordinate programs or projects within the portfolio. Managing risks at all levels is an active process involving continuous planning, analysis, response, monitoring, and control—always focusing on the adaptability, resiliency, and context of the organization.

3.2.3 Accountability at the Program Level

At the program level, evaluated risks span the related components and, if triggered, could have a positive or negative impact on one or more other components. Working with the component managers, it is the responsibility of the program manager to identify and manage any risks that could cause the program to be out of alignment with organizational strategy or the business model and objectives. Rather than manage these risks individually within the component, program managers should ensure that program risks are managed through coordination.

When managing strategic risk, program managers may identify new risks that exceed the organization's risk appetite and could directly impact the program. Strategic risks can present both threats and opportunities. Thus, the program manager evaluates and reviews a set of response options for consideration with the governance body. The program risk management strategy should include defining the risk thresholds applicable to the program- and component-level risks, performing the initial program risk assessment, and developing a high-level program risk response strategy.

Within a program, risks can affect the delivery of specific components. As a result, the program managers advise their component managers of any shared risks and response plans that relate to individual components. There may be economies of scale and scope in that the shared risks could be managed by initiating one risk response at the program level. The program manager should determine how the risk will be communicated to strategic levels of the organization, escalating the risk and issues appropriately within the program (component teams, program management team, program steering committee) and outside of it.

3.2.4 Accountability at the Project Level

At the project level, the objective of risk management is to (a) decrease the probability and impact of negative risks and (b) increase the probability and impact of positive risks specific to project deliverables or objectives. As defined in the *PMBOK® Guide* [2], the Uncertainty project management performance domain addresses activities and functions associated with risk and uncertainty. Project managers are accountable for evaluating, reporting, and managing both individual and overall project risks within the constraints of the project, proactively exploring and responding to uncertainty, anticipating threats and opportunities, and understanding the consequences of issues. The project managers may escalate certain risks to, or receive guidance from, sources such as the program manager, portfolio manager, project management office (PMO), governance board, and other leadership entities, depending on the complexity of the initiative and organizational inputs.

All project team members have responsibility for managing risks. These responsibilities could include the identification of risks, from initiation to closing; clarification of the trigger events; or awareness of potential new risks that could affect the endeavor. In addition, the members should manage uncertainty, which is inherent in all projects. The effects of any activity cannot be predicted precisely, and a range of outcomes can occur. The project manager, along with the project team, should implement strategies for responding to uncertainty including:

- **Gathering information.** Uncertainty can be reduced by finding out more relevant information with high reliability.

- **Preparing for multiple outcomes.** When there are only a few outcomes, the project team can prepare for each one, but when there is a large of set of potential outcomes, the project team should categorize and assess the causes, estimate the likelihood of occurrence, and focus on the most likely potential outcomes.

- **Set-based design.** Multiple designs or alternatives can be investigated early and validated progressively in the project to reduce uncertainty and eliminate poorer choices, while learning and adapting fast. This refers to an approach in engineering and product development where multiple design alternatives or concepts are explored and validated before narrowing them down to a single solution (see Figure 3-4). This method is applicable for projects with a high degree of uncertainty and allows for a broader exploration of possibilities, encourages creative thinking, and reduces the risks of prematurely committing to a single design. As more information becomes available, the set of options is gradually refined, leading to a well-informed and optimal final design decision.

- **Build in resilience.** The project team and project stakeholders should be able to learn, adapt, and respond quickly; for example, if the deadline for a minimum viable product (MVP) is moved up. The MVP is a concept used to define the scope of the first release of a solution to customers by identifying the fewest number of features or requirements that would deliver value. The team can self-organize and reprioritize work activities so more resources are allocated to the activities that will ensure the MVP is delivered at the earlier date.

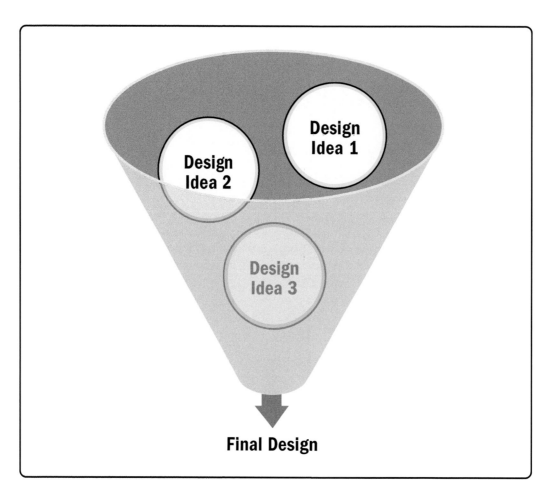

Figure 3-4. Set-Based Design Illustration

3.3 General Approaches to Risk Management

As risks are pervasive throughout portfolio, program, and project management activities, a systematic approach for managing risks is essential for the organization to achieve its strategic objectives. In this context of risk management, considerations include, but are not limited to, the following:

- Continuously evaluate events or circumstances that may occur in the future (their variability and ambiguity);

- Identify events that could have a positive or negative impact on one or more objectives of the enterprise, portfolio, program, or project;

- Assess the probability of the event occurring;

- Consider the impact of the event should it occur;

- Continuously monitor the overall portfolio, program, and project risks;

- Continuously manage the overall portfolio, program, and project risks with the aim of keeping risk exposure within an acceptable range;

- Continuously evaluate exposure to risk (opportunities and threats) to maximize positive impacts and minimize negative impacts;

- Engage with relevant stakeholders to understand their risk appetite and risk thresholds and coach or educate them on the importance of their roles in managing risks;

- Decide on an approach to respond to risks; and

- Compile the identified risks and manage them for future projects as lessons learned, as a contribution to the organization's risk management assets.

The specific processes for risk management are:

- Plan Risk Management,

- Identify Risks,

- Perform Qualitative Risk Analysis,

- Perform Quantitative Risk Analysis,

- Plan Risk Responses,

- Implement Risk Responses, and

- Monitor Risks.

For more details on the specific processes for risk management, refer to Section 4.

3.3.1 Factors for Evaluating Risk

Across the continuum of enterprise, portfolio, program, and project risk management, risks exist at all levels of the organization. Figure 3-5 provides a framework for classifying risks in one of four quadrants based on available information and the degree of ambiguity and variability. See Appendix X3 for more details on the classification of each quadrant. Evaluating risk aims to look at the impact on the organization should the risk occur and uses the outcome to determine whether the risk can be contained within the limits of the portfolio, program, or project capacity. Depending on the final determination, risk responses are selected and the risk register updated. Risk responses vary for the enterprise, portfolio, program, and project levels. More details will be supplied for each level in subsequent sections.

In order for risk management to take place, portfolio, program, and project managers should determine the risk probability and impact of each risk to determine the appropriate steps to respond:

- **Probability.** The chance of a risk occurring can range from slightly above 0% to just below 100%.

- **Impact.** Risks, should they occur, can have either a positive or negative consequence for the organization. The magnitude or significance of the impact may have varying implications and influences.

- **Compliance.** There may be legal or organizational obligations to meet some requirements.

There are additional factors to consider when evaluating risks. For a partial list of risk parameters, refer to Appendix X2.

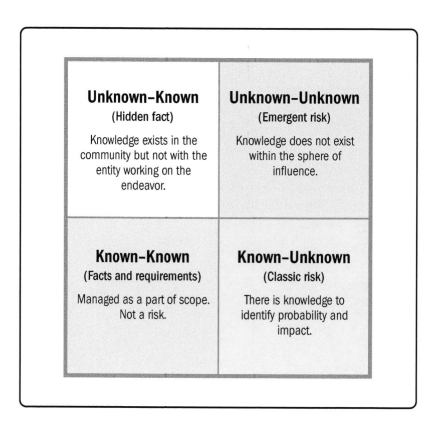

Unknown–Known (Hidden fact) Knowledge exists in the community but not with the entity working on the endeavor.	**Unknown–Unknown** (Emergent risk) Knowledge does not exist within the sphere of influence.
Known–Known (Facts and requirements) Managed as a part of scope. Not a risk.	**Known–Unknown** (Classic risk) There is knowledge to identify probability and impact.

Figure 3-5. Risk Classification

3.3.2 Responding to Risks

There are different approaches to responding to risks within portfolios, programs, or projects, depending on whether they are negative or positive. Options to consider for negative risks include:

- **Accept.** This option is available to both positive and negative risks and means the team accepts the risk. Acceptance could be passive or active. Passive acceptance does not require any other procedure other than documenting the risk and then leaving the team to handle the risk as it arises. With an active acceptance method, a contingency reserve is created to cover the loss of time, money, or other resources.

- **Avoid.** Threat avoidance is when the threat influences the behaviors and motivation of the team or stakeholders to avoid exposure to compromising events altogether.

- **Escalate.** This option is applicable to both positive and negative risks and should be chosen when the proposed response falls outside the defined scope or the team's influence or authority.

- **Mitigate.** In threat mitigation, action is taken to reduce the probability of occurrence and/or impact of a threat. Early mitigation is more cost-effective than trying to repair damage after the threat has occurred.

- **Transfer.** This option involves shifting the ownership of the risk to a third party to manage the risk and to bear the impact if the threat occurs.

Options to consider for positive risks include:

- **Accept.** This option is applicable to both positive and negative risks and is described under the options for negative risks.

- **Enhance.** The team acts to increase the probability of occurrence or impact of the opportunity. Risk enhancement is best done early in the endeavor.

- **Escalate.** This option is applicable to both positive and negative risks and is described under the options for negative risks.

- **Exploit.** The team acts in such a way as to ensure the opportunity occurs so they can take advantage of it and the portfolio, program, or project can reap the maximum benefits.

- **Share.** This option involves allocating part of the benefit of an opportunity to a third party that is better able to capture the opportunity.

Risk Management Life Cycle in Portfolio, Program, and Project Management

4

Organizations create adaptive frameworks to stay in sync with their competitive environments and tackle the growing complexities involved in achieving goals and making decisions. These complexities are inherent in portfolios, programs, and projects, as well as their surrounding environments, and are challenging to manage because of the various elements in the workflow: human behavior, system behavior, uncertainty, and ambiguity. Dealing with complexity affects the organization's stability, predictability, capacity, and ability to sustain its business activities.

For additional information about managing complexity in the project environment, refer to *Navigating Complexity: A Practice Guide* [5].

4.1 Introduction to the Risk Management Life Cycle

The risk management life cycle described in this section illustrates a structured approach for undertaking a comprehensive view of risk throughout the enterprise, portfolio, program, and project levels. Even though the way of managing risks differs at each level, and from one organization to another, an overall life cycle approach outlines a sequence of logical phases that can be iterated and includes the following processes:

- Plan Risk Management,
- Identify Risks,
- Perform Qualitative Risk Analysis,
- Perform Quantitative Risk Analysis,
- Plan Risk Responses,
- Implement Risk Responses, and
- Monitor Risks.

The risk management life cycle is shown in Figure 4-1. It has a dedicated, procedural, and iterative workflow of activities and processes that is integrated, supported, and performed across the enterprise and within the portfolio, program, and project levels. Because of the evolutionary nature of risk, the risk management life cycle ensures a repeatable sequence of processes fostering strategic decision-making.

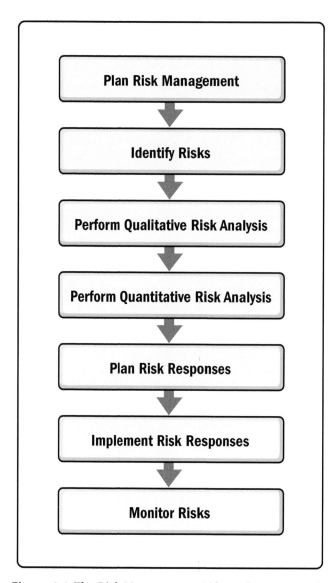

Figure 4-1. The Risk Management Life Cycle Framework

The iterative workflow of the risk management life cycle is embedded within a strategic execution framework where portfolio, program, and project management are linked to organizational cultural foundations, capabilities, and the use of organizational functions or performance domains. It is understood that once a portfolio, program, or project is closed, the risk management process terminates, and the appropriate lessons learned are documented. The framework enables the overall risk processes to be implemented through a risk management plan within portfolios, programs, and projects, as described in Sections 5, 6, and 7.

We will be referring to the following case study throughout this guide. More details of the case study will be shared as we go through further elaboration.

Case Study: Introduction to the Compact Wind Turbine Project

A regional municipality has embarked on an ambitious project, the Compact Wind Turbine Project, which aligns with the municipality's strategic objective to embrace sustainability, contribute to carbon neutrality, and promote regional development (see Figure 4-2). The efficient, ecofriendly wind turbines, already common in both developed and emerging economies, are set to empower rural and remote areas, aligning with the strategic objective.

As per the strategic plan, the wind turbines will supply sustainable energy to various sectors, including communities, businesses, schools, health clinics, individual households, and farms. The adaptable design allows these turbines to meet specific requirements, reinforcing the strategic focus on fostering local innovation while promoting global sustainability standards.

However, the project faces various risks, including design inconsistencies, technical difficulties, cost escalations, and regulatory challenges. Environmental uncertainties, such as unpredictable weather and potential supply chain disruptions, add to the complexity of the project risk landscape. Effective risk management is integral to aligning the project with the strategic vision.

Stakeholders

The stakeholder group is diverse and includes the municipality, the energy management department, local community members, environmental sustainability advocates, media representatives, the project manager, material suppliers, subcontracting agencies, and agricultural landowners.

Each stakeholder has a crucial role in managing project risks. Their contributions will be key to strategically driving the project toward its ultimate goal of promoting sustainable development and energy independence, thereby aligning the project with the municipality's broader strategic plan.

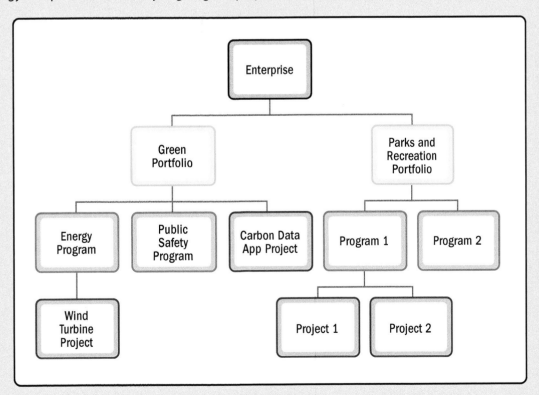

Figure 4-2. Portfolio Overview for the Municipality

4.1.1 Risk Management in Adaptive, Predictive, and Hybrid Project Management

In project management, risk management involves identifying, assessing, and prioritizing risks. Once this has been completed, the next step is to allocate resources to minimize, monitor, and control the likelihood or impact of negative events or to maximize opportunities.

However, organizations have the flexibility to choose from different project management approaches, each of which is guided by the same risk management steps listed previously. These approaches are adaptive, predictive, or hybrid. Each approach has its own strengths and weaknesses, and the selection depends on factors such as the specific project, the team involved, stakeholder preferences, and the organization's overall strategy.

In fast-paced and uncertain environments with an expectation of frequent changes, agile and other adaptive approaches tend to be more suitable. On the other hand, predictive approaches are better suited for stable projects with well-understood requirements and clearly defined outcomes. The decision on which approach to use should be based on a thoughtful assessment of the project's characteristics and the unique needs and circumstances of the organization.

The selection of a project management approach has a direct impact on how risks are managed throughout the project life cycle. The right choice should be made based on a careful evaluation of the project's unique characteristics and the level of uncertainty involved. To that end, effective risk management ensures that potential pitfalls are addressed proactively and that opportunities are maximized, ultimately leading to successful project outcomes.

4.1.1.1 Adaptive Project Management Approaches

Risk management is an integral part of the entire project life cycle in adaptive project management approaches such as Scrum, Kanban, or other kinds of agile practices. The approaches are designed to address and manage risk throughout the project, not just at the beginning during the planning phase. Also, high-level preliminary risk identification is required, although it may be at the release level and more detailed for the current sprint or iteration.

Early de-risking is achieved by using techniques such as "spikes," where risk is high and is used to expel identified uncertainties. Milestones, such as "stakeholder vision" and "proven architecture," further support effective risk reduction. Refer to *Choose Your WoW: A Disciplined Agile Approach to Optimizing Your Way of Working* [6] for more information.

The characteristics of risk management when using an adaptive approach to project management include:

- **Iterative approach.** The project is divided into small, manageable parts that can be completed in shorter increments or fixed periods of time. A project can also run quick iterations to implement gradual changes within the project while still meeting deadlines and deliverables. This allows risks to be identified and addressed early during individual iterations, so they can then be considered for future planning.

- **Continuous risk identification.** Because the team constantly reviews and adjusts their work, they can quickly identify and react to risks as they emerge. This real-time risk management can be much more effective than trying to predict all risks at the outset.

- **Flexibility.** In adaptive approaches to project management, changes are expected and embraced. This ability to change course quickly can help treat risks that could be more damaging in a rigid project structure.

- **Transparency.** Regular exercises such as standups, sprint planning, and retrospectives help identify risks and manage them early. They provide an opportunity for the team to discuss concerns and potential risks and produce strategies to manage them.

- **Frequent delivery and feedback.** Regular delivery of increments and subsequent feedback provide continuous improvement opportunities that help identify risks or issues early in the project and can minimize the impacts by taking corrective actions earlier.

4.1.1.2 Predictive Project Management Approaches

In predictive project management approaches, such as waterfall, the majority of risk identification usually occurs up front during the project planning phase while risk management continues throughout the life cycle.

The characteristics of risk management when using a predictive approach to project management include:

- **Initial risk identification.** In predictive models, the team attempts to identify high-level risks at the beginning of the project and continues to identify risks as the project progresses. This process involves using different techniques, e.g., SWOT (strengths, weaknesses, opportunities, threats) analysis, brainstorming, interviews, past projects, etc. All parties should be involved in the risk identification process to ensure the various perspectives and experiences are taken into consideration. The risks should be reviewed and evaluated based on the impact and likelihood of each risk. The risk identification should also include considering multiple outcomes and scenarios of each risk and the expected value and variance. Risks can be positive or negative. This process should be repeated periodically during the life of the project.

- **Structured risk management.** Risk management is usually structured, often with dedicated risk management roles and standardized processes.

- **Continuous monitoring.** Once risks are identified and response plans are in place, it is important that the risks and response plans are reviewed on a periodic basis to ensure any changes or new risks are taken into consideration as the project progresses. If this process is not completed, there is a risk of project delays or cost overruns.

- **Less frequent delivery and feedback.** In predictive approaches, feedback is generally obtained at longer intervals, such as at the end of a phase or the end of the project, which may make it hard to adjust the risk management strategies during the project.

4.1.1.3 Hybrid Project Management Approaches

Hybrid project management combines predictive and adaptive approaches for flexibility and structure in risk management. It strikes a balance between adaptability and predictability, making it ideal for projects with both defined and undefined aspects.

The characteristics of risk management when using a hybrid approach to project management include:

- **Initial risk identification and planning.** Similar to predictive models, hybrid models often involve an initial risk identification and planning phase. The team attempts to identify potential risks and creates a high-level plan to treat them.

- **Iterative development.** Similar to adaptive approaches, a hybrid approach also divides the project into smaller parts or iterations. This iterative development allows for risks to be assessed and addressed on a smaller scale before they can impact the larger project.

- **Flexibility and adaptability.** A hybrid approach allows for more flexibility than predictive models, meaning risks can be addressed as they emerge and plans can be adjusted as needed. Flexibility and adaptability in hybrid models can be beneficial when dealing with unknowns or changes in the project.

- **Structured risk management.** Although there is flexibility, hybrid models also incorporate structured risk management procedures from predictive models, including the maintenance of a risk register, and may have dedicated roles for risk management.

- **Transparency and communication.** Regular meetings and communication allow for continuous identification, assessment, and responses to risks. Transparency and communication in hybrid models can include elements from adaptive approaches, such as standups, sprint planning, and retrospectives, combined with more formal risk-reporting approaches from predictive models.

- **Regular review of risks.** The team routinely reviews and adjusts their risk strategies throughout the project. The regular review of risks can include updating the risk register, reviewing the effectiveness of risk responses, and adjusting plans as needed.

- **Feedback and learning.** Like adaptive approaches, hybrid approaches value learning and adaptation gained during each iteration. Feedback is gathered not only at the end of the project, but also at the end of each iteration. Feedback and learning can help to adjust risk strategies and improve over time.

4.1.2 Integrating Project Risk Management and Organizational Risk Management

This section highlights the importance of combining two critical aspects of risk management— project risk management and organizational risk management—to optimize business resilience and enhance project success rates.

The matryoshka, also known as nesting dolls, can provide a perfect metaphor for understanding the relationships among an organization's strategy, portfolios, programs, and projects, especially in the context of risk management (see Figure 4-3).

Think of the largest doll as the organization's overall strategy. This overarching strategy contains everything within it, as the largest doll contains all the other dolls. The strategy doll encapsulates the general risks the organization may face and sets the direction and tone for how risks should be managed across all areas.

Inside the strategy doll, you find the portfolio doll. The portfolio represents a collection of programs or projects grouped together to facilitate effective management to achieve strategic objectives (*The Standard for Portfolio Management* [3]). The portfolio doll is smaller than the strategy doll because its risk scope is more specific. However, it inherits the strategy doll's risk management direction. Portfolio-level risk management examines the collective risks of its constituent programs and projects, plus the risks that emerge from the interactions among them.

Next, nestled within the portfolio doll, is the program doll. Programs are groups of related projects managed in a coordinated way to obtain benefits and control not available from managing them individually (*The Standard for Program Management* [4]). Programs have more specific, tailored risks

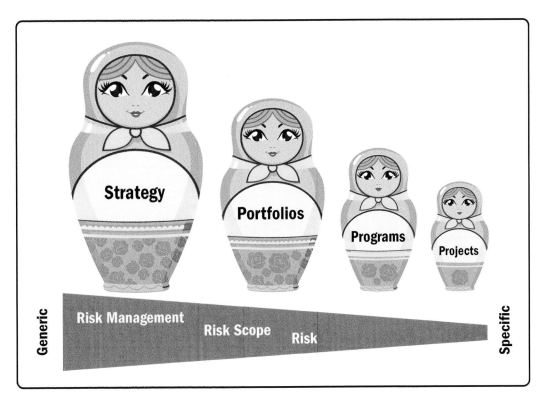

Figure 4-3. Integrating Project Risk Management and Organizational Risk Management

that align with their particular objectives. Program risks can come from individual projects but also from dependencies and interactions among projects.

Lastly, inside the program doll is the smallest doll—the project doll. Projects are temporary endeavors undertaken to create a unique product, service, or result. Each project has unique risks that should be identified, assessed, and managed. The project-level risks are the most granular, which entails looking at the specific risks that could derail a particular project.

In the same way that each doll is integral to the whole set of matryoshka dolls, each level of risk management—from the overall strategy to portfolios, programs, and finally, individual projects—is vital to the organization's overall success. This multilevel structure ensures a holistic approach to risk management that encompasses every level, from the broadest strategic risks down to the most specific project risks.

While project risk management is focused on identifying, analyzing, and counteracting potential risks that could impact specific projects—with the key objective of meeting project deliverables in terms of time, cost, and quality standards—organizational risk management aims to manage risks that affect the entire organization, such as the threats that could disturb the enterprise's strategic objectives, operational continuity, or reputation, expanding beyond the traditional project-centric view (see Figure 4-4).

This approach incorporates risk management considerations at different organizational levels beyond the completion of the project.

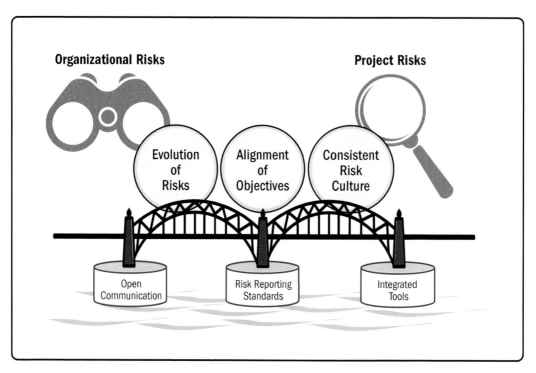

Figure 4-4. Primary Reasons for Integrating Project Risk Management and Organizational Risk Management

There are three primary reasons for integrating these two forms of risk management:

- **Evolution of risks.** Risks identified at the project level can evolve and impact the organization at large. Hence, connecting project risk management and organizational risk management practices can facilitate early risk detection and prevention.

- **Alignment of objectives.** Linking project risk management and organizational risk management ensures that project goals align with the broader organizational objectives, significantly contributing to the organization's overall success.

- **Consistent risk-focused culture.** Integrating project risk management and organizational risk management helps to cultivate a uniform risk culture. This promotes a clear understanding and effective organizational risk management engagement.

To facilitate this integration, employing the following strategies is recommended:

- **Open communication.** Fostering open and frequent communication among project managers and organization/enterprise risk managers aids in identifying and managing risks that could escalate and affect the organization. Communication can also help stakeholders in identifying secondary risks to their programs or projects resulting from organizational risk management activities happening outside of their programs or projects.

- **Risk management framework.** Establishing a comprehensive risk management framework that involves governance, risk reporting standards, controls, and compliance policies, as well as processes and procedures for execution and checking compliance, should be implemented at both the project and organizational levels.

- **Integrated risk management tools.** Incorporating a suite of tools designed to manage both project risk management and organizational risk management can help ensure consistent and effective risk management across the organization.

Understanding and implementing the integration of project risk management and organizational risk management is crucial for safeguarding both projects and day-to-day operations from unexpected risks. This comprehensive approach to risk management enhances the overall resilience of the organization by protecting projects and the entire organization from unforeseen challenges. To achieve this, a holistic view of risk management is necessary to establish the right structure within the organization's governance.

By creating the appropriate framework, the organization can clearly define its objectives and set external and internal parameters for an effective risk management life cycle. The risk management life cycle creation involves establishing risk criteria and processes iteratively, ensuring alignment with the organization's strategies and objectives while allocating resources effectively.

The risk management life cycle works within the risk management framework to ensure risks are managed in a structured manner—regardless of the portfolio, program, or project life cycle approach—and to avoid risks from escalating. Note that "structured" does not mean rigid. The structured process provides a systematic and organized approach to risk management, and the addition of flexibility ensures that the process remains relevant and effective in dynamic, unpredictable environments.

4.1.3 Risk Escalation

Risk escalation refers to the process of elevating the level of risk management from a lower level, such as a project or program, to a higher level, such as a portfolio or enterprise. It occurs when risks identified at a lower level have the potential to impact the broader scope and objectives of a higher-level entity.

At the project level, risk escalation involves identifying and assessing threats and opportunities that may affect the successful delivery of a specific project. These risks are typically managed within the project team and are primarily focused on achieving project objectives.

When risks escalate from the project level to the program level, they become risks that can impact the success of multiple related projects within a program. These risks are managed collectively, considering their interdependencies and potential impact on program-level objectives.

Further escalation occurs when risks are elevated from the program to the portfolio level. Risks at the portfolio level are strategic and can have implications for achieving organizational objectives. Considering the portfolio's overall risk appetite and strategic alignment, these risks are managed at a higher decision-making level.

In some cases, risks can escalate directly from a project or program to the enterprise level. These risks can potentially impact the entire organization and its overall performance, reputation, or strategic direction. Managing risks at the organizational level involves the highest level of decision-making and requires coordination across various portfolios, programs, and projects.

Effective risk escalation involves clear and timely communication, collaboration, and robust decision-making processes to ensure that risks are appropriately identified, assessed, and managed at the appropriate level of the organizational hierarchy. Appropriate risk escalation allows for a holistic view of risks, enabling proactive risk management strategies and informed decision-making to protect the organization's interests and optimize its overall performance.

Case Study: Risk Escalation in the Compact Wind Turbine Project

Using the case study provided earlier in this section, consider the following example of risk escalation:

Project level: The Compact Wind Turbine Project, at the project level, faces immediate risks such as design inconsistencies, technical difficulties, and potential supply chain disruptions. For instance, a technical difficulty could arise due to a fault in a turbine part, which would require immediate rectification to prevent project delays.

Program level: At the program level, this single project is part of a larger initiative aimed at promoting sustainable development and energy independence. Hence, any delay or cost overrun in this project could affect other projects in the program, such as creating energy storage facilities or implementing smart grid technologies. For instance, if supply chain disruptions lead to the delayed installation of wind turbines, it could postpone other interconnected projects.

Portfolio level: These programs are grouped under a broader portfolio aimed at embracing sustainability and contributing to carbon neutrality. Therefore, project- and program-level risk escalation can influence the portfolio. Using the previous example, delays in the Compact Wind Turbine Project and subsequent projects could push back the portfolio's timeline for achieving its sustainability targets.

Organization level: Finally, at the organization level, the municipality has an overarching strategy for regional development and carbon neutrality. As a result, significant risks at the portfolio level impact the entire organization's strategic objectives. Continuing with this example, the municipality may struggle to fulfill its strategic commitment to carbon neutrality within the planned timeframe if the delays in achieving sustainability targets are substantial.

4.1.4 Organizational Project Management and Its Application in Risk Management

The risk management life cycle, seamlessly incorporated into project management groups, consists of processes such as risk management planning, identification, qualitative and quantitative analysis, response planning, implementation, and monitoring. Implementation can differ across levels and organizations.

The models offer a two-dimensional framework for project management. One dimension depicts maturity levels, while the other highlights the key areas of project management. These areas are further divided into critical components for an accurate maturity assessment.

Although the models assess maturity in all project management areas, this section specifically delves into risk management maturity, enabling a thorough grasp of its practices and impact on project success. It should be noted that the levels of maturity outlined below may vary among organizational project management models.

4.1.4.1 Maturity Level 1: Initial Process

At the Level 1 stage, organizations are aware of project management processes but do not have standardized practices. There is no obligation for project managers to adhere to particular standards, and recordkeeping is inconsistent. The importance of project management is understood by management, but any data collection is sporadic and unstructured.

In the realm of risk management, organizations at this stage only achieve a minimal portion of the standards set by the risk management life cycle. Organizations may recognize the significance of risk processes, but their approach is casual, leading to potential gaps. Comprehensive risk management actions, from structured planning to ongoing monitoring, have not been integrated. Activities like maintaining organized risk logs, convening regular risk discussions, or creating structured response plans are lacking.

4.1.4.2 Maturity Level 2: Structured Process and Standards

At the Level 2 stage, organizations have implemented several project management processes. However, these are not uniformly accepted as organizational norms. There is documentation for these processes and management endorses their use, but a consistent understanding or enforcement across all projects is missing. Larger, more high-profile projects receive structured management and are typically more systematic. Basic metrics, such as cost, schedule, and performance, are tracked, though data may be gathered manually or in a piecemeal fashion. The information oscillates between being high level and very detailed.

In terms of risk management, Level 2 organizations exhibit greater maturity, but many key criteria remain unfulfilled. Level 2 organizations may, for instance, identify risks but may not have a consistent approach to quantify or address them. A comprehensive breakdown of these essential risk management success factors will be discussed later in this section.

4.1.4.3 Maturity Level 3: Organizational Standards and Institutionalized Process

At the Level 3 stage, every project management process is standardized across the organization. Clients play a crucial role in the project team, and almost all projects adhere to these standardized processes. Management has embedded these standards with comprehensive documentation available for all procedures. They actively participate in vital decisions, endorsing significant documents and addressing major project concerns. Automation is common in project management processes, and projects are evaluated in context with others. Regarding risk management, Level 3 organizations have solid and consistent processes. Activities like risk planning, identification, and evaluation align with organizational standards and promote comprehensive risk management. While they have standardized risk response plans and frequently review risk strategies, there is room for enhancement. To boost their risk management maturity, these organizations should develop action plans focusing on specific areas such as refining risk metrics or enhancing communication techniques.

4.1.4.4 Maturity Level 4: Managed Process

At the Level 4 stage, projects are overseen with insights from historical performance and future projections.

Management employs metrics for both efficiency and impact assessment on other projects. Every project, along with its changes and issues, is gauged using metrics derived from cost estimates, baseline predictions, and earned value. Project data syncs with other business systems to enhance decision-making. Established processes and standards aid in leveraging these metrics for informed project choices.

Management not only grasps its role in the project management process, it also adeptly oversees projects of various sizes and intricacies, discerning between general management styles and specific project requirements. Project management norms are harmonized with broader corporate systems and procedures. In terms of risk management, organizations at Level 4 have achieved most of the primary success markers for risk management.

Comprehensive change management facilitates integral risk oversight, driving informed business choices. For example, emergent project risks are monitored diligently, with swift updates provided to all pertinent parties. This ensures prompt, effective responses, diminishing any adverse effects. To further hone their risk management maturity, organizations should devise action plans that nurture and expand their proactive risk management ethos.

4.1.4.5 Maturity Level 5: Optimizing Process

At the Level 5 stage, processes are not only in place but are also actively used to boost project management tasks. Insights from previous projects are consistently analyzed and applied to refine project management methods, standards, and documentation. The organization, along with its management, is focused not just on effective project management, but also on ongoing enhancement. Metrics obtained during the project execution phase help guide understanding of individual project outcomes and shape broader organizational decisions.

Regarding risk management, Level 5 organizations embody a continual improvement mindset. Nearly all crucial benchmarks for the risk management life cycle are met at this optimized process stage, where risk management is seamlessly interwoven into project management activities. Risks are systematically pinpointed, evaluated, and addressed. Established protocols exist for observing these risks and adjusting strategies when required. Furthermore, Level 5 organizations perpetually refine their processes by drawing lessons from past projects, showcasing a deeply ingrained, forward-thinking approach to risk management.

4.2 Plan Risk Management

A comprehensive risk management strategy necessitates the formulation of a risk management plan. This plan outlines the execution of risk management processes and their integration with other processes. Essentially, it delineates the connections among risk management processes; overarching portfolio, program, or project management; and the organization's primary management practices. Risk management planning commences early in the overarching project planning phase, with its activities ingrained within the principal management strategy. This plan remains adaptable, adjusting to evolving work demands and stakeholder needs.

The practicality of such planning is influenced by the organization's characteristics. The stipulations set forth in the risk management plan echo the organization's culture; available resources; and underlying values, aims, and targets. This plan also pinpoints pertinent organizational practices, taking into account factors like strategic risk management, enterprise risk management, and corporate governance procedures.

4.2.1 Purpose of Plan Risk Management

The objectives of the Plan Risk Management process are to develop the overall risk management strategy, decide how the risk management processes will be executed, and integrate risk management with all other activities. The risk management plan defines both the normal frequency of repeating the processes and the specific or exceptional conditions under which the corresponding actions are initiated. The corresponding risk management activities are integrated into the portfolio, program, or project management plan.

4.2.1.1 Risk Appetite in Plan Risk Management

The level of risk that is considered acceptable depends on the risk appetites of the relevant stakeholders. A number of factors may affect stakeholders' risk appetites. These include the stakeholders' abilities to tolerate uncertainty and the relative importance of achieving specific objectives. The output of this analysis is then considered when applying the risk management processes.

Guidelines and rules for escalating risk-related information to management and other stakeholders reflect the stakeholders' risk appetites and expectations. As the work evolves, maintaining effective communication with the stakeholders enables portfolio, program, and project managers to become aware of any changes in the stakeholders' attitudes and adapt the risk management approach to take into account any new factors.

The risk management plan provides terminology for participants to share a common understanding of the terms. The risk management plan also defines the critical values of risk management and the thresholds that serve as parameters in a manner consistent with the scope of the work and the attitudes of the stakeholders. Similarly, the risk management plan specifies the key numerical values required in quantitative analysis or for decision-making in risk response planning or risk monitoring.

4.2.1.2 Tailoring and Scaling the Risk Management Plan

Portfolios, programs, and projects are exposed to different types of risk, so each step in the risk management life cycle is tailored and scaled to meet the various risk characteristics. The management processes are also tightly integrated among the portfolio, program, and project levels.

To ensure a shared understanding of the scope and goals of the risk management process, the stakeholders document, communicate, and then review the initial step's results.

The risk management plan includes tailored risk management processes that are based on the organization's process maturity. Scalable elements of the process that are part of risk management planning include but are not limited to:

- **Available resources.** Resources refer to both human resources and financial resources dedicated to risk management.

- **Escalation paths.** These paths include a detailed protocol for escalating identified risks throughout the portfolio, program, project, and organizational levels, depending on the risk severity.

- **Approaches and processes used.** Approaches and processes used may include regular risk assessment meetings, implementation of a risk register, or use of risk response strategies such as risk avoidance, transference, or acceptance, as will be discussed in further sections.

- **Tools and techniques used.** Tools and techniques refer to the specific risk management tools or software the organization uses to track and manage risks.

- **Supporting infrastructure.** Supporting infrastructure includes the systems and processes in place that aid in risk management.

- **Review and update frequency.** Review and update frequency refer to the frequency at which the risk management plan is reviewed and updated, keeping it relevant and effective.

- **Reporting requirements.** The reporting requirements refer to the specific requirements for reporting on risk management, including the type of information needed, the frequency of reports, and to whom they should be sent.

Case Study: Tailoring and Scaling the Risk Management Plan in the Compact Wind Turbine Project

In the Compact Wind Turbine Project, a specialized risk management team will determine which available resources may be allocated to the project, along with a dedicated budget to handle potential risk-related issues. The team may decide that no extra resources will be dedicated to the municipality's carbon-footprint-tracking web application development project, and the existing team will engage in the entire cycle of risk management.

When determining potential escalation paths for identified risks in the Compact Wind Turbine Project, a supply chain disruption risk may first be addressed at the project level, but if unresolved, it could be escalated to the program or even portfolio level.

When selecting which approaches and processes to use, the specific risk management strategies that the municipality applies will depend on the overall project management approach—adaptive, predictive, or hybrid.

One of the tools and techniques used in the Compact Wind Turbine Project includes a risk modeling software that could be used to predict potential cost escalations or project delays.

Supporting infrastructure for the project may include an integrated project management software system that helps monitor all aspects of the project, including the risk management activities.

The Compact Wind Turbine Project will also select its own risk review and update frequency. For example, risks could be reviewed weekly at team meetings and the plan could be updated quarterly.

From there, the project may decide to include risk updates in the monthly project reports that are sent to the municipality's energy management department.

These scalable elements ensure that the risk management plan is flexible and responsive to the changing project environment. Such elements will help the municipality's Compact Wind Turbine Project and other efforts stay aligned with its strategic objectives.

4.2.2 Key Success Factors for Plan Risk Management

The criteria for creating a valid risk management plan include:

- **Stakeholder acceptance.** For a risk management plan to be valid, it should be accepted by all key stakeholders. Regular meetings, public forums, or surveys could be used to ensure stakeholders understand and agree with the risk management approach.

- **Identification and correction of bias.** Any conscious or unconscious bias can skew the risk management process. Identifying and correcting these biases is important to ensure a fair and balanced approach. Including diverse perspectives, as well as holding facilitated workshops with a neutral facilitator to guide the discussion, helps ensure participation from all stakeholders and assists in challenging biased viewpoints to help correct bias.

- **Alignment with constraints and priorities.** The risk management plan should align with both internal and external constraints and priorities.

- **Balance of cost, effort, and benefit.** A successful risk management plan maintains a balance between the cost and effort of implementing risk response strategies and the expected benefits.

- **Completeness with respect to risk management process needs.** The plan should fully address the requirements of the risk management process, from risk identification and assessment to response planning, implementation, and monitoring.

Case Study: Planning Risk Management in the Compact Wind Turbine Project

In the case of the municipality, creating a valid risk management plan will involve considering the key factors as they relate to the Compact Wind Turbine Project.

Stakeholder acceptance should come not only from municipal officials and staff, but also community members, local businesses, and other relevant entities that may be impacted by the sustainability initiative.

Planning will also involve the identification and correction of any biases about the Compact Wind Turbine Project. If an assessment overemphasizes the potential financial risks while underemphasizing the environmental risks, this bias needs to be identified and corrected to help ensure a balanced sustainability focus.

To align with the municipality's constraints and existing priorities, the Plan Risk Management process should consider any budget constraints as well as the municipality's priority to reduce carbon emissions. These factors should also be considered when developing the risk management plan for all of the portfolios, programs, and projects that correspond to the municipality's strategic objective to embrace sustainability and contribute to carbon neutrality.

The Compact Wind Turbine Project's risk management planning should focus on achieving a balance of the cost, effort, and benefits of the project. The municipality's investment in renewable energy sources may have high up-front costs and require substantial effort, but the long-term benefits in terms of reducing emissions and energy costs should also be factored into the risk management plan to determine an appropriate balance.

In an effort to achieve completeness with respect to the Plan Risk Management process needs for the Compact Wind Turbine Project, the municipality should consider risks related to location, species endangerment, long-term maintenance, potential health impacts, and community engagement, among other factors.

4.3 Identify Risks

Once the risk management scope and objectives are agreed upon, the process of identifying risks begins, with care taken to distinguish genuine risks from nonrisks, such as concerns and issues. It is unlikely that all risks are, or even should be, identified at the outset. Over time, the risk exposure level may change due to the decisions and actions taken previously as well as externally imposed changes.

4.3.1 Purpose of Identify Risks

The purpose of risk identification is to identify key risks to the extent practicable. The emergent nature of risk requires the risk management process to be iterative, repeating the risk identification activities to find risks that were not previously evident.

Various risk identification techniques are available, each with their own strengths and weaknesses. One or more techniques can be selected, as appropriate, to meet the needs of a specific portfolio, program, or project. The aim is to expose and document all known risks, recognizing that some are inherently unknown and others will emerge later in the work. Input is sought from a wide range of stakeholders when identifying risks, since each stakeholder may have a different perspective on the risks facing the portfolio, program, or project. Historical records and documents may also be reviewed to help identify risks.

When a risk is first identified, preliminary responses may be identified at the same time. These are recorded during the Identify Risks process and considered for immediate action when appropriate. When such responses are not implemented immediately, they should be considered during the Plan Risk Responses process.

All identified risks are recorded and a risk owner may be identified at the same time. The risk owner is the individual responsible for monitoring the risk and selecting and implementing an appropriate risk response strategy. The risk owner's responsibility is to manage the corresponding risk throughout the subsequent risk management processes.

4.3.2 Key Success Factors for Identify Risks

Success in achieving the objectives of the Identify Risks process includes but is not limited to the following steps:

- **Early risk identification.** This step encompasses the proactive process of identifying potential risks at the beginning of a project. Organizations can take preventive measures to minimize negative consequences or to capitalize on opportunities by identifying risks early on. The benefits include proactive risk management, effective resource allocation, and stakeholder engagement.

- **Iterative risk identification.** This step entails the ongoing process of adapting to the nature of the project and involves identifying risks throughout the project life cycle on a continual basis, considering the project's specific characteristics. This approach allows for the discovery of new risks and adjustments to risk management strategies as the project progresses. The iterative identification of risks based on the nature of the project ensures that risk management remains dynamic and adaptable to the project's unique circumstances. Iterative risk identification facilitates a proactive approach to risk management, allowing project teams to address emerging risks in a timely manner and increase the chances of project success.

- **Comprehensive risk identification.** This step involves using multiple techniques and relevant stakeholders to identify key risks thoroughly. These techniques may include but are not limited to premortem brainstorming sessions, documentation review, expert interviews, assumptions analysis, reviewing lessons learned, SWOT (strengths, weaknesses, opportunities, threats) analysis, checklists, simulations, and scenario analysis. Organizations can use various approaches to capture a wide range of potential risks and develop a more robust risk management plan.

- **Explicit identification of opportunities and innovation.** This step involves actively recognizing and capturing positive events or circumstances that can benefit a project and includes identifying and leveraging technological advancements like artificial intelligence (AI), large language models (LLM), and machine learning (ML); forming strategic partnerships; improving processes; and capitalizing on competitive advantages. Organizations can proactively seek opportunities to enhance project outcomes and gain a competitive edge.

- **Multiple perspectives with high confidence.** High confidence in risk identification requires involving diverse stakeholders, who bring different insights and expertise. This approach ensures comprehensive risk coverage, enhanced risk understanding, increased accuracy, and stakeholder engagement, improving overall risk management strategies and project success.

- **Connecting risks to objectives.** This step involves linking identified risks to project objectives, helping organizations to prioritize risks, inform decision-making, develop targeted risk responses, and measure progress. This approach ensures that risk management efforts align with strategic goals, leading to successful project outcomes.

- **Complete risk statement.** To ensure effective risk identification, a complete risk statement is required because it enhances clarity, facilitates prioritization, supports risk response planning, and enables effective communication. Clear risk statements aid in understanding and managing risks, leading to improved project outcomes. An example of an effective risk statement would be one that captures the event, cause, and impact.

- **Risk ownership.** This step ensures accountability for managing risks while providing a high level of detail and enhancing risk assessment and response planning. Together, they contribute to proactive and comprehensive risk management, while mitigating potential impacts on project success. Having a risk owner means having someone dedicated to managing risk, which includes assessing it thoroughly and ensuring appropriate response planning. Risks can be identified by anyone, but assigning an owner to a specific risk will ensure they own it, are accountable for it, and provide the right amount of detail in order to manage it effectively.

- **Frequent and effective communication.** Frequent and effective communication is crucial for successful risk management. It involves timely updates, transparent information sharing, stakeholder engagement, risk-related discussions, and proper reporting. By prioritizing communication, organizations enhance risk awareness, enable informed decision-making, and nurture a collaborative risk management culture.

- **Objectivity to minimize bias.** Biases in projects can affect risk management. Examples include confirmation bias, where individuals favor information that confirms their beliefs; availability bias, which focuses on easily recalled information; anchoring bias, which relies heavily on initial data; and overconfidence bias, where individuals underestimate risks due to excessive confidence. Being aware of these biases helps promote objectivity in risk assessment and decision-making.

Case Study: Identifying Risks in the Compact Wind Turbine Project

In the Compact Wind Turbine Project, early risk identification involves conducting workshops to identify risks, assess and prioritize them, document them in a risk register, monitor and review them, and develop response plans.

In the municipality's carbon-footprint-tracking web application, the initial risk identification may focus on technical risks, such as compatibility issues, or application vulnerabilities, such as security breaches. However, as the project advances and user requirements evolve, new risks related to user acceptance or scope changes may emerge. By iteratively identifying risks based on the changing nature of the project, the project team can effectively manage and respond to these evolving risks.

4.4 Perform Qualitative Risk Analysis

Qualitative risk analysis evaluates the importance of each risk to categorize and prioritize individual risks for further attention. It also provides a mechanism for evaluating the level of overall portfolio, program, or project risk.

Qualitative risk analysis typically involves techniques such as risk probability and impact assessment, risk ranking or scoring, risk matrix analysis, and expert judgment. These techniques provide a qualitative understanding of the risks, allowing for initial decision-making and the identification of risks that require further quantitative analysis or more detailed risk assessment.

By performing qualitative risk analysis, organizations can gain valuable insights into their risk landscape, focus their attention on high-priority risks, develop appropriate risk management strategies to respond to potential threats, and explore opportunities.

4.4.1 Purpose of Perform Qualitative Risk Analysis

Qualitative techniques are used to assess individual risks. Qualitative techniques consider a range of characteristics, such as probability or likelihood of occurrence, degree of impact on the objectives, manageability, timing of possible impacts, relationships with other risks, and common causes or effects.

Assessing individual risks using qualitative risk analysis evaluates the probability that each risk, if it occurs, will have an impact on the portfolio, program, or project objectives. As such, this assessment does not directly address the overall risk resulting from the combined effect of all risks and their potential interactions. This can, however, be achieved through the use of quantitative risk analysis techniques.

Qualitative risk analysis is applied to the list of risks created or updated by the Identify Risks process to provide management with the characteristics of the risks that have the most influence (positive or negative) on achieving the objectives. Risks that are assessed as high priority, and that either threaten or enhance the achievement of objectives, are highlighted in the Plan Risk Responses process. These risks may be further analyzed using quantitative risk analysis.

4.4.2 Key Success Factors for Perform Qualitative Risk Analysis

Success in achieving the objectives of the Perform Qualitative Risk Analysis process includes but is not limited to:

- **Use an agreed-upon approach.** Establishing a standardized approach for conducting qualitative risk analysis is essential. This approach ensures consistency and allows for comparability across different projects or situations. Having an agreed-upon approach helps in understanding and assessing risks in a systematic, uniform manner.

- **Use agreed-upon definitions of risk terms.** In risk analysis, it is important to understand the terminology and use it clearly. The meaning of risk-related terms such as probability, impact, likelihood, and severity should be well defined and agreed upon by all stakeholders involved. Consistent and shared definitions help facilitate effective communication and accurate risk assessment.

- **Collect credible information about risks.** To perform a qualitative risk analysis, gathering relevant and reliable information about the identified risks is necessary. This information can be obtained through various means, such as interviews, surveys, historical data, industry reports, and expert opinions. Collecting credible information ensures the accuracy and validity of the risk analysis process.

- **Perform iterative qualitative risk analysis.** Qualitative risk analysis is not a one-time activity, but is an iterative process involving continuous risk evaluation and reevaluation. It is important to revisit and review the risk analysis periodically to update and refine the assessment based on new information or changes in the project environment. The iterative analysis allows for the identification of emerging risks, the reassessment of existing risks, and the adjustment of risk response strategies accordingly.

4.5 Perform Quantitative Risk Analysis

The Perform Quantitative Risk Analysis process provides insight into the combined effect of identified risks on the desired outcome. This process takes into account probabilistic or component-wide effects, such as the correlation among risks, interdependencies, and feedback loops. The process provides an indication of the degree of overall risk faced by the portfolio, program, or project.

4.5.1 Purpose of Perform Quantitative Risk Analysis

The Perform Quantitative Risk Analysis process provides a numerical estimate of the overall effect of risk on the objectives. Results from this analysis are used to evaluate the likelihood of success in achieving objectives and to estimate any contingency reserves.

Analyzing uncertainty using quantitative techniques provides a more realistic estimate than a nonprobabilistic approach. However, quantitative risk analysis is not always required or possible. Therefore, during the Plan Risk Management process, the benefits of quantitative risk analysis should be weighed against the effort required to ensure that the additional insights and value justify the additional effort.

A partial risk analysis, such as a qualitative risk analysis, prioritizes only individual risks and therefore does not produce measures of overall risk where all risks are considered simultaneously.

Calculating estimates of overall risk is the focus of the Perform Quantitative Risk Analysis process. Specific risks are usually best understood and quantified at a detailed level. In contrast, objectives are specified at a higher level. An overall risk analysis using quantitative techniques helps estimate the implications of all quantified risks. Thus, a thorough understanding of individual risks and their relative importance to objectives enhances quantitative risk analysis and the subsequent assessments of risks. The overall risk may determine the priority that should be placed on specific risks.

Estimating overall risk using quantitative methods helps distinguish the quantified risks that threaten objectives beyond the stakeholders' tolerance from those risks that are within acceptable tolerances, even when the risk is considered. The risks that threaten objectives beyond the stakeholders' tolerance may be targeted for vigorous risk responses aimed at protecting the objectives that are most important to the stakeholders.

4.5.2 Key Success Factors for Perform Quantitative Risk Analysis

Success in achieving the objectives of quantitative risk analysis includes but is not limited to:

- **Effective prior risk identification and qualitative risk analysis.** These are preliminary steps where potential risks are identified and qualitative analysis is performed to understand their impact and probability. This analysis forms the basis for the later quantitative risk analysis and gives it a solid starting point. This step allows for an early stage of understanding risks, their nature, and their potential effect on the project or process.

- **Appropriate model.** Quantitative risk analysis requires statistical models to project potential outcomes based on the identified risks. Selecting an appropriate model is crucial, as it forms the basis of quantitative risk analysis. The model should accommodate all identified risks and their interrelationships and provide accurate, understandable results.

- **Competence with the corresponding technical analysis tools.** The tools used for analysis should be in line with the model chosen. Users should be competent with these tools to ensure accurate results. This step may require training or hiring staff with the necessary expertise.

- **Commitment to collecting credible risk data.** Reliable, accurate, and comprehensive data form the backbone of quantitative risk analysis. The data collected should be based on comprehensive and unbiased facts. Commitment to this process ensures the quality and validity of the results.

- **Unbiased data.** The data used in quantitative risk analysis should be objective and unbiased. Any bias in the data could lead to skewed results, undermining the value and accuracy of the risk analysis.

- **Understanding interrelationships among risks in quantitative risk analysis.** Risks are often not isolated and may be interconnected. Understanding these interconnections is critical, as it can provide insights into how risks can compound or interact. This insight forms a more holistic view of the risk landscape and allows for more accurate modeling and forecasting.

4.6 Plan Risk Responses

The Plan Risk Responses process determines the appropriate response actions for the priority of the individual risks and the overall risk. This process takes into account the stakeholders' risk attitudes and the conventions specified in the risk management plan, in addition to any constraints and assumptions that were determined when the risks were identified and analyzed. Once individual risks have been prioritized, appropriate risk responses are developed for both threats and opportunities. This process continues until an optimal set of responses has been developed. A range of possible responses exists for both threats and opportunities.

Five responses may be considered for dealing with threats:

- **Escalate.** Escalation is appropriate when a threat is outside of the portfolio, program, or project scope or when the proposed response exceeds a given manager's authority. Escalated risks are managed at the enterprise, portfolio, or program level, or other relevant parts of the organization. The relevant party in the organization accepts ownership of escalated threats. A threat is usually escalated to the appropriate level that matches the objective that would be affected if the threat occurred.

- **Avoid.** Risk avoidance is when the portfolio, program, or project team acts to eliminate a threat or protect an activity from any impact of risk realization. This strategy may be appropriate for a high-priority threat with a high probability of occurrence and a large negative impact. Avoidance may involve changing some aspect of the risk management plan or changing the objective that is in jeopardy in order to eliminate the threat's impact entirely. Should the risk materialize, it would have no effect on the objective. The risk owner may also take action to isolate the objective from the risk's impact if it were to occur.

- **Transfer.** Transference involves shifting the responsibility of a threat to a third party to manage the risk and bear the impact if the threat occurs. Risk transference often involves the payment of a risk premium to the party taking on the threat.

- **Mitigate.** In risk mitigation, action is taken to reduce the probability of a threat's occurrence and/or impact if the threat occurs. An early mitigation action is often more effective than trying to repair the damage after the threat has occurred. Where it is not possible to reduce the probability, a mitigation response may reduce the impact by targeting factors that drive the severity.

- **Accept.** Risk acceptance acknowledges the existence of a threat; however, no proactive measures are taken. This strategy may be appropriate for low-priority threats or when it is not possible or cost-effective to address a threat in any other way. Acceptance can be either active or passive. The most common active acceptance strategy is to establish a contingency reserve, including amounts of time, money, or other resources, to handle the threat if it occurs. Passive acceptance involves no proactive action aside from a periodic review of the threat to ensure that it does not change significantly.

Case Study: Responses to Threats in the Compact Wind Turbine Project

In the case study, the five responses to threats could entail the following:

- **Escalate.** The municipality may identify a threat related to the broader environmental impact of the wind turbine project, such as potential harm to local bird populations. This threat may be outside the project's scope or exceed the project manager's authority. In this case, the threat may be escalated to a higher level in the organization such as the environmental department or a regulatory body. This higher authority would then take ownership of and manage the threat

(Continued)

appropriately. For instance, the environmental department may conduct a thorough impact assessment and develop a mitigation plan to protect local bird populations. By escalating the threat to the appropriate level, the municipality can ensure that it is properly managed and that the potential impact on the project objectives is minimized.

- **Avoid.** The municipality may identify a high-priority threat of regulatory challenges that could halt the Compact Wind Turbine Project. To avoid this risk, they may decide to change some aspects of the project management plan to eliminate the threat entirely. For instance, they may decide to use a different, approved model if the regulatory bodies do not approve a particular type of wind turbine. This strategy would help ensure that the project can proceed without the risk of regulatory challenges, thereby isolating the project objectives from the impact of this risk.

- **Transfer.** The municipality may identify the threat of technical difficulties in the operation of the wind turbines. To transfer this risk, they could contract with a third-party service provider specializing in wind turbine maintenance and repair. This third party would then be responsible for managing the risk of technical difficulties and would bear the impact if such difficulties occurred. In return, the municipality would pay a risk premium to the service provider, which could be a fixed fee, a percentage of the project budget, or some other form of compensation. This arrangement would allow the municipality to focus on other aspects of the project while ensuring the technical difficulties are properly managed.

- **Mitigate.** The municipality may identify the threat of design inconsistencies in the wind turbines. To address this threat, they could take early action, such as implementing rigorous quality control checks and standardizing design processes, to reduce the probability of inconsistencies occurring. If it is not possible to completely eliminate the probability of design inconsistencies, stakeholders could focus on reducing the impact. For instance, they could establish a dedicated team to quickly address any design issues that arise, thereby minimizing the impact on the overall project timeline and budget. This strategy would target the factors driving the threat's severity, such as project implementation delays or cost overruns.

- **Accept.** In the Compact Wind Turbine Project, active and passive acceptance of threats could entail the following:

  o **Active acceptance**: The municipality may acknowledge the threat of unpredictable weather affecting the operation of the wind turbines. However, due to the inherent nature of weather, they may not take immediate action to prevent this risk. Instead, they could establish a contingency reserve of funds to be used for maintenance or repairs if severe weather damages the turbines. They could also develop a contingency plan to execute should such an event occur.

  o **Passive acceptance**: The municipality may recognize the threat of potential supply chain disruptions due to global economic conditions or other external factors. However, due to the complexity and unpredictability of these factors, they may decide not to take immediate action. This typically occurs when the cost to remediate a threat is higher than the anticipated benefit of that remediation. Instead, they could periodically review the threat, keeping track of changes in the global economy or the stability of their suppliers that could increase the risk of supply chain disruptions.

Five responses may be considered for dealing with opportunities:

- **Escalate.** This risk response strategy is appropriate when an opportunity is outside the portfolio, program, or project scope or when the proposed response exceeds a given manager's authority. Escalated opportunities are managed at the portfolio or program level or by other relevant parts of the organization. It is crucial that the appropriate party in the organization accepts ownership of an escalated opportunity. Opportunities are usually escalated to the level that matches the objectives that would be affected if the opportunity occurred.

- **Exploit.** The exploit strategy may be selected for high-priority opportunities where the organization wants to ensure that the opportunity is realized. This strategy seeks to capture the benefit associated with a particular opportunity by ensuring that it definitely happens, increasing the probability of its occurrence to 100%.

- **Share.** Sharing involves allocating ownership of an opportunity to a third party so that the third party shares some of the benefit if the opportunity occurs. It is important to carefully select the new owner of a shared opportunity to ensure the capture of the opportunity for the benefit of the portfolio, program, or project. Risk sharing often involves the payment of a risk premium to the party taking on the opportunity.

- **Enhance.** This strategy is used to increase an opportunity's probability and/or impact. Early enhancement action is often more effective than trying to improve the benefit after the opportunity has occurred. The probability of occurrence of an opportunity may be increased by focusing attention on its causes. Where it is not possible to increase the probability, an enhancement response may increase the impact by targeting factors that drive the size of the potential benefit.

- **Accept.** Accepting an opportunity acknowledges its existence, although no proactive action is taken. This strategy may be appropriate for low-priority opportunities and may also be adopted where it is not possible or cost-effective to address an opportunity in any other way. Acceptance can be either active or passive. The most common active acceptance strategy is establishing a contingency reserve—including amounts of time, money, or other resources—to take advantage of the opportunity, or the development of a contingency plan, which could be implemented if it appears that the opportunity is being realized. Passive acceptance involves taking no proactive action aside from a periodic review of the opportunity to ensure that it does not change significantly.

Case Study: Responses to Opportunities in the Compact Wind Turbine Project

In the case study, the five responses to opportunities could entail the following:

- **Escalate.** The municipality may identify an opportunity to expand the Compact Wind Turbine Project to other regions or sectors currently outside of the project scope. For example, they may see an opportunity to use wind turbines to power public transportation systems or to sell surplus energy to other municipalities. However, this plan may exceed the project manager's authority or the current project scope. In this case, the opportunity could be escalated to a higher level in the organization such as the regional government or the energy department. It is important that the escalated opportunity be accepted by the relevant party. For instance, the regional government may need to approve the expansion of the project, or the energy department may need to agree

(Continued)

to manage the sale of surplus energy. By escalating the opportunity to the appropriate level, the municipality can ensure it is properly managed and the potential benefits are realized.

- **Exploit.** The municipality may identify the opportunity to use wind turbines to contribute to carbon neutrality as a high-priority opportunity. To exploit this opportunity, the municipality could take action to ensure that it occurs. For instance, the municipality could invest heavily in the Compact Wind Turbine Project, ensuring that enough turbines are installed and operational to meet their carbon neutrality goals. They could also prioritize this project in their strategic planning, allocate sufficient resources, and engage key stakeholders to help ensure its success. By doing so, the municipality increases the probability of occurrence to 100%, ensuring that the benefits associated with this opportunity, such as reduced carbon emissions, energy independence, and alignment with global sustainability standards, are fully realized.

- **Share.** The municipality may identify an opportunity to share the benefits of the Compact Wind Turbine Project with a third party such as a private energy company or a nonprofit organization focused on sustainable energy. For example, they could transfer the ownership of some turbines to this third party. In return, the third party could share some of the benefits if the opportunity arises, such as a portion of the energy produced or the profits from selling the energy. This could help the municipality spread the costs and risks associated with the project, while also ensuring the benefits of the project are realized. However, this likely involves the payment of a risk premium to the third party taking on the opportunity. This could be a fixed fee, a percentage of the profits, or some other form of compensation. The municipality would need to carefully select the new owner to ensure that the opportunity is captured for the benefit of the project and aligns with their strategic objectives.

- **Enhance.** The municipality may identify an opportunity to enhance the impact of the wind turbines by tailoring them to meet the specific requirements of different sectors. For instance, they could focus on the causes that would increase the probability of this opportunity, such as investing in research and development to improve the adaptable design of the turbines. To enhance the impact, the municipality could target factors that drive the size of the potential benefit. For example, they could collaborate with local businesses, schools, health clinics, and farms to understand their specific energy needs. By customizing the turbines to meet these needs, the municipality could increase the impact of the project, leading to greater energy savings and more widespread adoption of sustainable energy solutions. This strategy could enhance the project's benefits and align with the municipality's strategic objective of promoting regional development and sustainability.

- **Accept.** In the Compact Wind Turbine Project, active and passive acceptance of opportunities could entail the following:

    o **Active acceptance**: The municipality may acknowledge the opportunity to use the wind turbines to promote local innovation. However, they may not take immediate action due to budget constraints or other priorities. Instead, they could establish a contingency reserve of funds to be used when the opportunity becomes more feasible. For instance, they may set aside a portion of the budget to invest in research and development or training programs to foster local innovation when the time is right.

    o **Passive acceptance**: The municipality may recognize the opportunity to use wind turbines to supply sustainable energy to various sectors like schools, health clinics, and farms. However, due to the complexity of the project and the risks involved, they may decide to avoid taking immediate action. Instead, the municipality could periodically review the opportunity, keeping track of changes in technology, market demand, or the regulatory environment, which could make it more feasible or attractive in the future.

Responses are planned at a general, strategic level, and the strategy is validated and agreed upon prior to developing the detailed tactical approach. Once that is accomplished, the responses are expanded into actions at the tactical level and integrated into the relevant management plans. This activity may generate additional secondary risks that may need to be addressed at this time.

In addition to individual risk responses, actions may be taken to respond to the overall portfolio, program, or project risk. All response strategies and actions are documented, communicated to key stakeholders, and incorporated into the relevant plans.

4.6.1 Purpose of Plan Risk Responses

The Plan Risk Responses process aims to determine the set of actions that provides the highest chance of success while complying with applicable constraints. Once risks have been identified, analyzed, and prioritized, plans are developed for addressing each risk that the team considers sufficiently important, either because of the threat it poses to the objectives or because of the opportunity it offers. The plans describe the agreed actions to be taken and the potential changes that these actions may cause.

Risk responses, when implemented, can have potential effects on the objectives and, as such, can generate additional risks. These are known as secondary risks and are analyzed and planned for in the same way as those initially identified. There may be residual risks that remain after the responses are implemented. These residual risks are clearly identified, analyzed, documented, and communicated to all relevant stakeholders continuously until they are satisfied.

4.6.2 Key Success Factors for Plan Risk Responses

Success in achieving the objectives of the Plan Risk Responses process includes but is not limited to the following:

- **Clearly define roles and responsibilities for implementing risk responses.** This clarity helps everyone involved in the project to know their role when it comes to managing risks. This includes knowing who is responsible for identifying, assessing, and responding to risks and who has the authority to make decisions about risk responses.

- **Specify the timing of risk responses.** This task helps determine when risk responses should be implemented. Some risks may require immediate action, while others can be addressed at a later stage in the project. By specifying the timing of risk responses, risks can be addressed in a timely manner and resources can be used efficiently. Some risks, like design inconsistencies or technical difficulties, should be addressed immediately to prevent delays in the project. Other risks, like potential supply chain disruptions, can be addressed as they arise. The project manager should specify the timing of these responses to ensure efficient use of resources.

- **Provide resources, budget, and a schedule for responses.** This task helps to allocate sufficient resources (including time, money, labor, and materials) to implement the risk responses. This allocation may involve setting aside a contingency budget for dealing with risks or scheduling extra time in the project management plan to deal with potential issues.

- **Address the interaction of risks and responses, considering secondary and residual risks.** This task helps to consider how different risks and responses may interact. For example, a response to one risk could inadvertently increase another risk (a secondary risk), or there may be some level of risk that remains even after the response has been implemented (a residual risk). Considering these interactions assists in developing more effective and comprehensive risk responses. Additionally, some level of risk may remain even after a response to environmental uncertainties has been implemented. The project manager should consider these interactions when planning risk responses.

- **Ensure appropriate, timely, effective, and agreed-upon responses.** All relevant stakeholders should agree that risk responses are suitable for the risks they are designed to address. Responses should also be implemented in a timely manner to effectively reduce the risk. This ensures that everyone is on the same page and that risk responses are as effective as possible.

- **Address both threats and opportunities.** Addressing both threats and opportunities reiterates the fact that not all risks are negative. Some risks may present opportunities that could benefit the project if managed correctly. By addressing both threats and opportunities, potential issues can be prevented while also pursuing and taking advantage of potential benefits.

Case Study: Planning Risk Responses in the Compact Wind Turbine Project

Clearly defined roles and responsibilities for implementing risk responses are key considerations in planning risk responses for the Compact Wind Turbine Project. Each project stakeholder has a crucial role in managing project risks as they arise. For example, the municipality is responsible for regulatory compliance, the energy management department oversees technical aspects, and local community members are involved in monitoring environmental impacts.

Then, with the specific timing of the identified risk responses determined, the municipality should allocate sufficient resources to manage the risks. The municipality may need to set aside a contingency budget to deal with cost escalations or schedule extra time to deal with potential regulatory challenges. When other potential secondary or residual risks may arise in the project, it is important to consider how these risks may interact with other risks. For example, addressing the risk of design inconsistencies with the wind turbine may inadvertently increase the risk of cost escalations in the project. Consideration of all of the potential interactions helps to determine more effective and comprehensive risk responses as additional risks arise. The municipality should continue to ensure that the appropriate, timely, effective, and agreed-upon risk responses are in place to manage these risks.

To help ensure alignment, all of the relevant stakeholders of the Compact Wind Turbine Project, including the municipality, the energy management department, local community members, and others, should agree on the risk responses. For example, the response to regulatory challenges should be suitable for the risk, implemented in a timely manner to effectively reduce the risk, and then agreed upon by all relevant stakeholders.

While the projects included in the case study face various negative risks or threats, they also present positive risks or opportunities. For example, the adaptable design of wind turbines could foster local innovation and promote global sustainability standards. By managing this risk effectively, the municipality can take advantage of this potential benefit and further align the project with its strategic objectives.

4.7 Implement Risk Responses

Once the planning of risk responses is complete, all of the approved unconditional response actions should be included and defined in the relevant management plans. These actions may be delegated to response owners as appropriate. The risk owner monitors actions to determine their effectiveness and to identify any secondary risks that may arise because of the implementation of risk responses.

The risk owners and risk response owners should be briefed on any changes that may affect their responsibilities. Effective communication should be maintained between the risk owners and the portfolio, program, or project managers so that the designated stakeholders (a) accept accountability for controlling the potential outcomes of specific risks, (b) apply their best efforts to track the associated trigger conditions, and (c) carry out the agreed responses in a timely manner.

In addition to the response actions and trigger conditions, a mechanism for measuring the effectiveness of the response should be provided as part of the risk response planning. The risk response owner should keep the risk owner aware of the status of the response actions. The risk owner should then decide whether the risk has been effectively dealt with or if additional actions should be planned and implemented. This ensures the agreed-upon actions are carried out within the normal portfolio, program, or project execution framework.

4.7.1 Purpose of Implement Risk Responses

The Implement Risk Responses process aims to carry out the agreed-upon risk response actions should the risk occur. Proper attention to the Implement Risk Responses process helps to ensure the agreed-upon risk responses are executed accordingly.

4.7.2 Key Success Factors for Implement Risk Responses

Success in achieving the objectives of the Implement Risk Responses process includes but is not limited to:

- **Assigned risk ownership.** Each identified risk should have an accountable owner who is responsible for its management. For instance, technical difficulties may be assigned to the project's lead engineer, while regulatory challenges could fall under the jurisdiction of a compliance officer.

- **Stakeholder commitment.** It is essential that all stakeholders are on board with the planned risk responses.

- **Effective communication management.** Clear and regular communication helps to ensure that everyone is informed regarding risk management efforts. For instance, weekly risk management updates could be circulated among the project team, while monthly reports could be sent to a wider stakeholder group.

- **Cost determination.** The estimated costs of risk responses should be calculated and incorporated into the overall project planning. For instance, the cost of additional inspections to manage technical difficulties should be factored into the project budget.

- **Availability of reserves.** Adequate contingency and management reserves should be set aside to address any risks that materialize. For example, a contingency reserve could be allocated to cover potential cost escalations, while a management reserve may be used to address unforeseen regulatory challenges.

Case Study: Implementing Risk Responses in the Compact Wind Turbine Project

When a risk occurs in the Compact Wind Turbine Project, such as the design-inconsistency risk discussed earlier, the previously identified risk response owner (or owners) for the design inconsistencies should manage that risk.

All of the stakeholders responsible for implementing the risk response should be committed to ensuring that the risk is addressed as required. If the risk response involves altering the design of the turbines, the design team, materials suppliers, and potentially even local regulatory authorities should commit to implementing these changes.

To help ensure alignment among the stakeholders, effective communication should be in place, including risk management updates and reports that keep everyone informed about the risk management activities needed to address the design inconsistencies.

The municipality should keep track of the costs associated with addressing the design-inconsistency risk and should budget and plan for the risk to help ensure it is managed appropriately. If necessary, contingency and management reserves can be allocated to cover any potential cost escalations that may result from altering the design or materials, or the associated regulatory requirements that may arise.

4.8 Monitor Risks

The Monitor Risks process enables the portfolio, program, or project management team to reevaluate the status of previously identified risks; identify new emergent, secondary, and residual risks; and determine the effectiveness of the risk management processes.

The portfolio, program, or project environment may change as some risks occur, whether foreseen or unforeseen, and other risks become relevant or cease to be relevant. The management team should ensure the planning documents are kept current as additional information becomes available. Periodic risk reassessment using the risk management life cycle should be repeated at reasonable intervals or in response to relevant events.

In the event of major organizational changes, risk management planning may need to be revisited prior to performing a risk reassessment.

In addition to regular status reviews, periodic risk audits should be performed to determine strengths and weaknesses in handling risks within the portfolio, program, or project. The audits entail identifying any barriers to effectiveness or keys to success in risk management that could help improve the risk management of current or future portfolios, programs, or projects (see Figure 4-5).

At the end of the program or project, an integrated analysis of the risk management process should be carried out with a focus on long-term process improvements. This analysis consolidates lessons learned that are applicable to a large proportion of the organization's future programs or projects, such as appropriate levels of resources, adequate time for the analysis, use of tools, level of detail, etc.

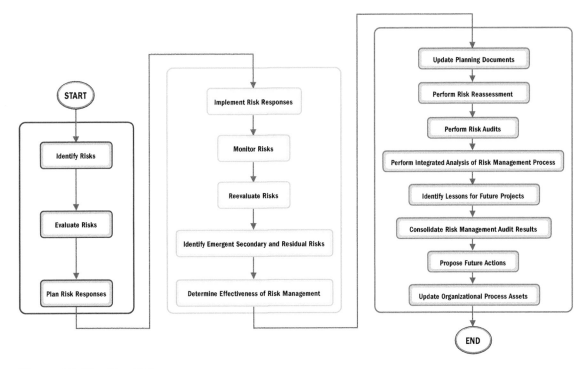

Figure 4-5. Monitor Risks

The results of the risk management process audit are consolidated with specific information with respect to the experience of risk in the portfolio, program, or project. The results are highlighted, and potential future actions are proposed for applying them. These potential future actions may include any generally applicable guidelines for the organization, and the results can lead to an update of the corresponding organizational process assets.

4.8.1 Purpose of Monitor Risks

The primary objectives of the Monitor Risks process are to track identified risks and maintain the viability of response plans. In addition to tracking and managing the risk response actions, the effectiveness of all of the risk management processes should be periodically reviewed to provide improvements to the management of the current work as well as future work with an activity such as capturing lessons learned.

The corresponding set of trigger conditions is specified for each risk or set of risks for which a contingent response has been defined. The risk owner is responsible for ensuring that these conditions are effectively monitored and that the corresponding actions are carried out as defined in a timely manner.

4.8.2 Key Success Factors for Monitor Risks

The key success factors for the monitoring of risks include but are not limited to:

- **Integrated risk monitoring.** It is essential to have a cohesive approach toward risk monitoring that integrates all areas of the project. For example, tracking technical difficulties should be coordinated with monitoring potential supply chain disruptions to help ensure a comprehensive view of the project's risk landscape.

- **Continuous monitoring of risk trigger conditions.** Regularly assessing conditions that could trigger risks helps to preempt potential issues. Assessment involves a review of the defined potential causes to ensure they are still valid and/or to determine if new ones may have arisen.

- **Maintaining risk awareness.** An ongoing awareness of potential risks among all stakeholders can facilitate proactive risk management. Maintaining risk awareness could be achieved through regular risk management briefings to the project team, sponsors, steering committees, and wider stakeholder groups such as local community members and environmental sustainability advocates.

Case Study: Monitoring Risks in the Compact Wind Turbine Project

When a risk is identified in the Compact Wind Turbine Project, the municipality should work to ensure that the project takes a consistent approach toward monitoring that risk for all areas of the project. For instance, the team should closely monitor weather patterns to help prepare for any potential environmental uncertainties that may affect the installation of the turbines. The monitoring of this risk should include the assessment of any identified trigger conditions, such as a local weather alert, and should continuously review whether these conditions are accurate or if any new issues may arise.

5

Risk Management in the Context of Portfolio Management

Realizing the organization's strategic objectives is the goal of risk management at the portfolio level, which aims to secure efficient and effective value delivery. Combining the management of opportunities and threats helps to achieve this goal.

At the portfolio level, risk management considers the entire organizational framework. A portfolio is a collection of subsidiary portfolios, programs, projects, and operations managed as a group to achieve strategic objectives. Risk management at the portfolio level ensures that all of the components implement consistent and effective processes to manage the entire risk management life cycle.

One of the main goals of portfolio management is to build a risk-efficient portfolio where the organization chooses to take an appropriate amount of risk within the portfolio to achieve the required value in the overall organizational strategy. Based on their contributions to the overall risk exposure and strategic importance, portfolio components are either added or removed to realize this goal.

5.1 Interconnectedness of Risks in Portfolios, Programs, and Projects

The intricacies of portfolio risk management become evident when considering that risks, programs, and projects are intertwined components of larger systems such as portfolios. This interconnectedness necessitates a comprehensive understanding and management of risks at various levels. This section explores the concept of risk efficiency in the context of portfolio risk management.

5.1.1 Risk Efficiency and Risk-Return Trade-Offs

Within the context of portfolios, risk efficiency is a powerful mechanism for attaining a harmonious balance between risk and reward. It is crucial to recognize that engaging in low-risk projects, while seemingly advantageous, could yield minimal rewards. This could potentially undermine the value of the investment made in a project within the portfolio. As a result, a minimum internal-return-on-investment threshold becomes evident, which needs to be achieved to make the project's undertaking worthwhile within the portfolio.

In portfolio management, as a manager's goal for bigger profits grows, the risk tied to the projects in the portfolio also increases. This suggests that there is a limit to how much risk is acceptable. This limit marks the point beyond which the risk of the projects in the portfolio gets too high, no matter how big the potential profits. So, the balance of risk and reward creates a range within the portfolio, from projects with low risk and low reward to those with high risk and high reward.

Case Study: Portfolio Management in the Context of the Compact Wind Turbine Project

To illustrate, in the context of portfolio management for the municipality case study, consider the green portfolio. This portfolio aims to pursue environmentally friendly initiatives and includes diverse projects like an energy program, a public safety program, and a municipal carbon-footprint-tracking web application development project.

(Continued)

As the municipality's desire for larger benefits from this portfolio grows—combined with a desire for greater energy savings, an increase in carbon neutrality targets from the wind turbine project, increased safety from the public safety program, and more accurate carbon data from the app project—the risk associated with these projects also increases. There is a limit to how much risk the municipality can take on from these projects, beyond which the consequences of failure become too severe, regardless of the potential benefits.

For instance, a delay in the implementation of the wind turbine project could lead to a delay in energy savings and meeting goals. A flaw in the public safety program could result in ineffective measures for improving the municipality's safety goals. An error in the carbon-data-tracking project could cause incorrect data collection and usage, potentially leading to incorrect decisions.

This balance of risk and reward creates a spectrum within the green portfolio, ranging from projects with low risk and low reward, like minor updates to the public safety program, to those with high risk and high reward, such as implementing an entirely new wind turbine project. This spectrum helps the town decide how to allocate resources and manage the projects in its portfolio.

5.1.2 Risk Exposure in Portfolios

A portfolio can comprise a diverse mix of subsidiary portfolios, programs, projects, and business-as-usual operations. Within such a portfolio, maintaining a balance of risk exposures is key. This includes engaging in low-risk projects that assure predictable outcomes (albeit with minimal rewards) and high-risk projects that provide the potential for significant returns (accompanied by higher risk levels). To achieve a risk-efficient portfolio, it should neither be overly exposed to excessive risk nor underexposed, which would limit the potential rewards.

5.1.3 Role of Portfolio Manager

The efficacy of a risk-efficient strategy hinges mainly on the portfolio manager's ability to accurately gauge each portfolio component's inherent riskiness. Determining the expected rewards is a comparatively straightforward task, given that these are derived from the predicted benefits and objectives of the programs and projects. However, computing the overall portfolio's risk exposure necessitates a consistent risk assessment process. For a more detailed explanation on the role of the portfolio manager, in general, refer to *The Standard for Portfolio Management* [3].

5.1.4 Risk-Efficient Boundary and Organizational Strategy

An organization's overarching strategy and its risk appetite significantly influence the risk-efficient boundary (i.e., defining acceptable levels of risk and reward based on the expected effectiveness of the risk treatment). Alterations to key strategies will invariably cause shifts in risk exposure, necessitating subsequent readjustments in the portfolio components.

Managing risk in the portfolio is not something that is done as frequently as in projects due to the longer timeframes of portfolios. This widens the life cycle of risk management.

Case Study: The Risk-Efficient Boundary in the Compact Wind Turbine Project

For instance, the wind turbine project or the public safety program could take years to complete. As a result, adjustments to the portfolio, such as adding or removing projects, may only happen once or twice a year.

Still, it is crucial for the municipality to regularly and consistently assess the risks associated with the components in the portfolio and how well they match the expected balance of risk and reward. For example, if the wind turbine project faces significant delays and cost overruns, it may no longer align with the municipality's risk-reward expectations. Regular check-ins can help ensure the portfolio's health and determine if it is still helping the municipality meet its green objectives and carbon neutrality targets.

5.1.5 Emerging Trends in Portfolio Risk Management

The continuous evolution and understanding of risk management can offer interesting insights into new application areas and potential contributions to various disciplines. Portfolio management is an emerging field that promises innovative applications and further developments in risk management approaches.

There are several emerging trends in portfolio risk management:

- **Artificial intelligence (AI) and machine learning (ML).** Both AI and ML are increasingly being used to predict and manage portfolio risks. Advanced algorithms can analyze large amounts of information from previous portfolios, programs, and projects using their internal databases as well as external, real-world data within the public domain. This use of advanced algorithms enables risk managers to identify patterns more quickly and accurately. These tools can help portfolio managers identify hidden risks, anticipate market changes, and make more informed decisions. (Note: This practice guide is meant to be read in general terms. There are many other publications and case studies available to become more familiar with how AI works.)

- **Robotic process automation (RPA).** RPA can be a powerful tool for portfolio risk management, enhancing efficiency and accuracy while minimizing human error. RPA aids in automating risk identification and assessment by scanning portfolio components' data and flagging potential issues based on predefined criteria, enabling early mitigation. Furthermore, it facilitates continuous monitoring of key project indicators and generates automatic risk reports, aiding proactive risk management. RPA can also streamline risk prioritization across the portfolio components by processing extensive risk data and categorizing the risks based on their potential impact, optimizing resource utilization. Additionally, RPA can assist in implementing response plans and ensuring compliance with relevant regulations, thus reducing the risk of noncompliance.

- **Cyber risk management.** As digital transformation accelerates, managing cyber risk has become crucial to portfolio risk management. Understanding and managing these cyber risks is essential, as any cyber threat could seriously impact the performance of the portfolio.

- **Environmental, social, and governance (ESG) risk management.** Portfolio managers are increasingly incorporating ESG risk assessments into their risk management strategies, looking at environmental factors like a company's carbon footprint, social impact, and corporate governance practices. There is growing recognition that ESG factors can significantly impact the requirements of a project and, subsequently, a portfolio's performance.

- **Stress testing and scenario analysis.** In reaction to economic uncertainties, the use of stress testing and scenario analysis is gaining traction in portfolio management. These techniques can aid portfolio managers in anticipating how their portfolios may fare under different challenging conditions.

- **Integrated risk management.** Although not necessarily emerging, integrated risk management is being more widely applied, which necessitates a comprehensive view of all of the risks across a portfolio and their interactions. Understanding these interconnected risks provides a more accurate assessment of the portfolio's overall risk profile. This holistic view enables managers to develop more robust risk mitigation strategies that account for the interplays among different projects within the portfolio.

Case Study: Incorporating Emerging Trends in the Compact Wind Turbine Project

In the Compact Wind Turbine Project, the municipality wants to ensure that they are considering the impact of the portfolio on the community as well as incorporating some of the emerging tools and techniques available to assist with their risk management efforts.

The municipality is exploring the use of AI and ML to support data analysis and the making of informed decisions. The use of AI and ML will assist in finding patterns in the portfolio more quickly and accurately, which can help to identify hidden risks, monitor risk indicators, and make more informed decisions using data from previous portfolios, programs, and projects. The use of RPA will help categorize any identified risks based on their potential impact, which can help to determine how resources should be allocated in the portfolio.

The municipality is also embracing digital transformation, particularly through projects like the carbon data app in its green portfolio. Managing cyber risk has become a vital aspect of the municipality's portfolio management. The municipality's portfolio managers need to evaluate the cybersecurity measures in place for their projects, especially those with significant digital components. For instance, the carbon data app project will require robust cybersecurity measures to protect the collected and processed data from potential cyber threats. Understanding and managing these cyber risks is essential, as any cyber threat could seriously impact the performance of the portfolio (e.g., a cyber breach in the carbon data app could disrupt operations and negatively affect public trust in the municipality's initiatives, potentially derailing other projects in the portfolio).

The portfolio manager, who is overseeing the municipality's green portfolio, is progressively incorporating ESG risk assessments into the risk management strategy. For instance, the portfolio manager may consider the environmental impact of wind turbines and other similar projects within the initiative that directly address the portfolio's carbon footprint. The portfolio manager should evaluate the social impact of projects and programs like the public safety program, which aims to improve safety and well-being in the community. The portfolio manager may also scrutinize governance practices, such as how decisions are made for the carbon data app project, ensuring transparency and accountability.

The municipality's green portfolio manager may perform a stress test on the wind turbine project to see how it would cope with unexpected changes in funding or significant increases in material costs. Scenario analysis could be used for the public safety program, examining its resilience in various situations, like a rise in local crime rates or a natural disaster. For the carbon data app project, the municipality may explore scenarios related to data security breaches or sudden shifts in regulatory requirements. Understanding these potential scenarios helps the portfolio manager to make necessary adjustments, reinforcing the resilience of the portfolio against diverse adverse conditions.

An integrated risk management approach could become increasingly relevant for the municipality's green portfolio. By adopting this approach, the portfolio manager can understand how the risks associated with the wind turbine project, for example, may impact the public safety program or the carbon data app project. For instance, if the wind turbine project runs over budget, it may affect the available funds for other projects. Alternatively, if the carbon data app project faces a data breach, it may impact public trust and participation in the public safety program.

It is in the interest of the municipality to take these emerging considerations into account and to evaluate new tools and techniques to help ensure that the portfolio is implementing a robust yet measured approach to their risk management activities.

5.2 Portfolio Risk Management Life Cycle

The risk management life cycle, as described in Section 4, generally applies to portfolio management. Several additional considerations for the corresponding processes should be considered in this context, as outlined in this section.

5.2.1 Portfolio Risk Identification

Risk identification at the portfolio level is focused on (a) identifying the risks that have an impact on the delivery of the expected business performance and (b) the ability of the organization to implement its strategy and achieve its strategic objectives.

There are two levels of risk:

- **Strategic risks.** Strategic risks are identified directly at the portfolio level and triggered by portfolio activities. Strategic risks include activities related to business performance by the portfolio components and those impacting the organization's ability to achieve its strategic objectives.

- **Tactical risks.** Tactical risks are short-term risks that are either raised by management procedures at the portfolio level or originate from the portfolio's components.

Risks that can impact portfolio components typically include the following categories:

- Changing business needs, environment, or context;
- Availability of resources;
- Interactions among components; and
- Conflicting component objectives.

Case Study: Strategic-Level Portfolio Risks in the Compact Wind Turbine Project

Based on the definition of strategic-level risks, and reviewing the case study provided in Section 4, here are a few examples that could be considered strategic-level portfolio risks:

- **Market volatility.** Changes in market conditions, such as fluctuations in energy prices or shifts in government policies, can impact the financial viability of the wind turbine portfolio.

- **Regulatory changes.** Shifts in regulations or policies related to renewable energy and sustainability could introduce compliance risks or alter the economic incentives for the portfolio.

- **Technology obsolescence.** Rapid advancements in wind turbine technology could render the existing portfolio outdated or less competitive, leading to potential obsolescence risks.

- **Investment viability.** The portfolio may face a risk related to the financial viability of the Compact Wind Turbine Project. Factors such as budget constraints, cost escalations, or inadequate return on investment could impact the overall business performance and the portfolio's ability to achieve its strategic objectives.

- **Reputation and public perception.** The municipality's reputation and public perception could be at risk if the Compact Wind Turbine Project faces challenges, controversies, or negative impacts on the environment or local communities. Maintaining a positive reputation is crucial for achieving strategic objectives and ensuring ongoing support for sustainability initiatives.

5.2.2 Portfolio Risk Qualitative and Quantitative Analyses

The evaluation of risks at the portfolio level is performed by considering the impact of risks on the realization of the expected business performance or the execution of the organizational strategy. One of the reasons these analyses are conducted is to evaluate whether the level of impact can be contained within the scope of the portfolio manager's accountability.

When the impact affects the portfolio's business performance or strategic objectives, then the impact is typically addressed at the portfolio level operationally. When the impact affects the ability of the organization to execute strategy and realize the intended value, the risk—and responsibility to respond to the risk—are escalated to a higher governance level.

Case Study: Portfolio Risk Analyses in the Compact Wind Turbine Project

In the case study, for example, evaluating risks at the portfolio level involves assessing the effect of these risks on the expected performance of the municipality's green initiatives or the overall environmental strategy. The purpose of these assessments is to determine whether the impact of these risks falls within the responsibility of the portfolio managers overseeing the green portfolio.

For example, if a risk, such as a delay in the wind turbine project, affects the performance of the green portfolio, this risk would typically be managed tactically at the portfolio level. The portfolio managers may respond by adjusting project timelines, reallocating resources, or revising project objectives.

However, if the impact of a risk, such as a major budget overrun or a significantly negative public response to the carbon data app, threatens the municipality's ability to execute its broader environmental strategy and realize the intended value of its green initiatives, the risk and the responsibility to address it would be escalated to a higher governance level such as the city council or the mayor's office. The risk would then be managed at this higher level, potentially involving strategic decisions like revising the overall portfolio or the municipality's broader strategy.

5.2.3 Portfolio Risk Response Strategies

In portfolio risk management, risk responses focus on exploiting business opportunities and maximizing value creation for the organization and its stakeholders. It goes beyond treating threats, which, at the portfolio level, are merely limitations to actions. Portfolio management also includes responding to risks escalated by its components to ensure that these are effectively and efficiently addressed at the appropriate level.

In principle, all the potential responses listed in Section 4 can be used when responding to risks at the portfolio level.

The risk response strategies developed at the portfolio level consist of the activities documented in the portfolio risk management plan. In addition, some responses are developed because of escalation at the component level. These activities are budgeted accordingly and funded from the relevant sources. Examples of relevant funding sources are the portfolio or component's budget for preventive responses, relevant contingency reserves for handling occurrences of known risks, or management reserves for handling unforeseen risk-related issues.

Risk responses can be planned as additional portfolio components such as subsidiary portfolios, programs, projects, or elements of the portfolio governance framework. These components are aimed at maximizing business performance or enhancing the execution of organizational strategy to achieve strategic objectives. In some cases, the risk response can also lead to removing components from the portfolio.

5.2.4 Implementing Portfolio Risk Responses

The implementation of risk responses within a portfolio includes:

- Triggering risk responses as they have been defined in the portfolio risk management plan,

- Transferring the corresponding budget from the management and contingency reserves into the budget at completion, and

- Updating the portfolio baselines accordingly.

The risk responses planned as new components become part of the portfolio and are subject to the application of the standard portfolio delivery and deployment processes.

Any formally approved risk response is integral to the portfolio management plan. Implementing such a response is not a change to the portfolio initiated through a formal portfolio change management procedure. However, any new responses planned to address emergent risks become part of the portfolio change management procedure.

5.2.5 Monitoring Portfolio Risks

Monitoring risks at the portfolio level is both a strategic and tactical activity, described as follows:

- **Strategic activity.** Monitoring risks strategically addresses the evolution of the risk characteristics of each portfolio component, the overall portfolio risk profile, and the impact of that evolution on business performance. The focus is on the development and implementation of the organizational strategy and the achievement of strategic objectives. These risk profiles are regularly analyzed in order to identify any potential trends that may indicate new risks or the inefficiency or ineffectiveness of the response strategies. The monitoring of risk responses is conducted according to quantitative parameters and qualitative assessments. These risk responses are intended to effectively treat the specific risk they are addressing to enhance or maintain the realization of the expected business performance and the execution of the organizational strategy. The qualitative assessment is performed by revising the risk analysis to ensure these plans are efficient and effective. Finally, it is critical to ensure the portfolio's components are properly implemented and that effective, risk-related elements of the governance framework are part of the monitoring of risks at the portfolio level.

- **Tactical activity.** Monitoring risks tactically oversees the aspects related to the execution of the anticipatory and responsive actions undertaken to respond to identified risks. Tactical monitoring also ensures that operational or systemic risks that could impact the portfolio are properly handled.

5.3 Integration of Risk Management into the Portfolio Management Performance Domains

In order to achieve the portfolio objectives, several risk management practices can be applied across the portfolio life cycle within all of the performance domains (see Figure 5-1). These practices typically cover the areas shown in Table 5-1.

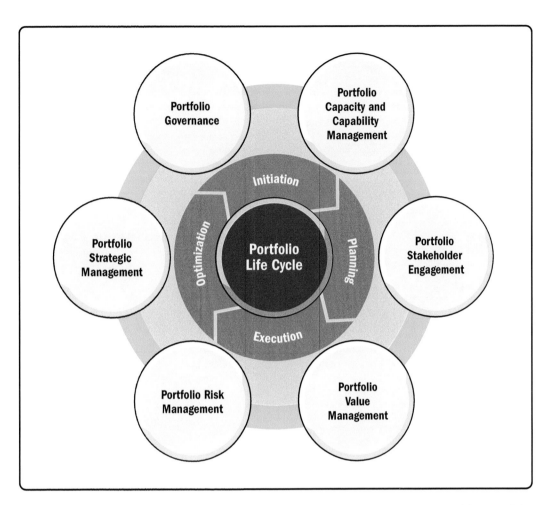

Figure 5-1. Portfolio Management Performance Domains (Source: *The Standard for Portfolio Management* [3]**)**

Table 5-1. Areas of the Portfolio Management Performance Domains Typically Covered by Risk Management Practices

Performance Domain	Areas Covered by Risk Management Practices
Portfolio Strategic Management The essence of Portfolio Strategic Management is to ensure the enhancement or exploitation of strategic opportunities and the avoidance or mitigation of threats that could potentially prevent the organization from achieving its full potential. Therefore, risk management in the context of portfolio strategic management focuses on identifying and actively managing those opportunities and threats that could substantially impact the realization of the organizational strategy.	• Alignment with the organization's risk attitude and strategy • Quality of the organization's strategy • Impact of strategic changes within the organization • Interpretation of the portfolio mission, vision, strategic goals, and objectives • Impact of external opportunities and threats
Portfolio Governance The purpose of Portfolio Governance is to ensure that the portfolio is managed in an appropriate way. This includes meeting the legal, regulatory, and organizational governance requirements. The role of risk management within portfolio governance is to use the organization's potential to (a) efficiently secure adequate governance and management practices and (b) avoid or address threats that could lead to misconduct or ineffective management of the portfolio.	• Portfolio governance structures, policies, and procedures • Assignment of individuals to key governance roles • Risk-based audits • Use of audit reports
Portfolio Capacity and Capability Management Risk management in the context of Portfolio Capacity and Capability Management focuses on the mutual impact of the portfolio and related operations. In addition, risk management in the context of capacity and capability management ensures the proper use and development of capital and assets entrusted to the portfolio manager for the component programs and projects.	• Impact of the portfolio on other activities in the organization • Impact of other activities within the organization • Key human, financial, and intellectual capital • Availability and fit for the use of the key assets • Capacity required to manage risk • Impact of the organizational culture, structure, and key processes • Capacity of the partners and suppliers • Use of performance reports • Impact of portfolio optimization on value delivery
Portfolio Stakeholder Engagement Key stakeholders at the portfolio level typically include executive leaders and managers of the organization and their equivalents in the key partner, supplier, and customer organizations. Another key group of stakeholders is the component managers. From this perspective, portfolio risk management focuses on (a) opportunities to increase the effectiveness of realizing the organization's strategy and (b) threats that could potentially lower the ability to do so.	• Methods for stakeholder identification, categorization, and analysis • Attitude of key portfolio stakeholders • Interactions and conflicts of interest • Ways of engaging stakeholders • Scope, channels, techniques, and frequency of communications
Portfolio Value Management Portfolio Value Management focuses on ensuring that the investment in portfolio components leads to the delivery of expected value. In this context, risk management focuses on (a) maximizing opportunities to increase the value delivered and (b) responding to threats that could potentially lower the value or probability of value delivery.	• Opportunities to increase value delivery • Trends in the portfolio environment • Alignment of value targets with risk attitudes • Impact of component risks on value delivery • Approach to the expected value negotiations
Portfolio Risk Management Portfolio Risk Management focuses on ensuring that risk at the portfolio and its component levels is recognized and managed effectively. It is achieved through risk management and governance practices. Because these practices are essential for dealing with uncertainty at the portfolio level, they are also analyzed from a risk perspective. Adequate measures are then taken to ensure that the application of risk management is robust and effective.	• Risk management approach • General portfolio risks • Cumulative effects of component risks • Risk escalation policies

Risk Management in the Context of Program Management

6

Risk management in program management is a strategic effort aimed at optimizing program benefits while navigating complexity, addressing potential threats, and seizing opportunities. This strategic effort involves the integrated management of both positive and negative risks.

Programs comprise a collection of interconnected projects, subsidiary programs, and coordinated activities. This program-level coordination generates benefits that are unattainable when such components are managed in isolation. Additionally, programs include operational activities related to completed program components, which can generate or be influenced by risks. Thus, risk management ensures efficient processes for managing the entire risk life cycle of these program components.

6.1 Distinctions and Challenges in Program Risk Management

The primary goal of program risk management is to address uncertainties that may impact program objectives. This distinction is crucial, as programs have different strategic focuses and desired outcomes compared to individual projects. Acknowledging these differences and implementing appropriate risk management approaches helps organizations overcome program-specific uncertainties, align with strategic goals, and enhance program success.

6.1.1 Understanding Program Risk Management

As indicated earlier, risk management at the program level is strategic, aiming to optimize benefits while mitigating threats and uncertainties and taking advantage of opportunities. Programs, due to their complex nature, blend various projects and subsidiary programs, resulting in synergistic benefits when managed holistically (see Figure 6-1).

6.1.2 Sources, Nature, and Types of Program Risks

Programs face multifaceted risks from individual projects, the portfolio level, and internal complexities. Furthermore, risks can be categorized via projects, program-level coordination, overarching program aspects, and strategic-level decisions. Risks also can be classified as overall (affecting the entire program) and individual (specific events or conditions influencing individual components). Risks can be categorized as follows:

- **Risks escalating from projects.** Some project risks may exceed project-level scope and require program-level management, stemming from factors like scope changes, delays, resource limitations, technical difficulties, or stakeholder conflicts. Diligent monitoring and evaluation of key project risks are essential to respond to escalation and help ensure program success.

- **Emerging risks at the program level.** These risks involve coordination, resource allocation, dependency management, and technology sharing among program components. They also could pertain to program management, execution, control, reporting, alignment with strategic objectives, and changes in requirements. Managing these overarching risks is crucial for program success.

- **Risks cascading from the portfolio and strategic levels.** Changes in organizational strategies, policies, or external factors can introduce new risks or alter the existing risk landscape for programs. Identifying and assessing these strategic-level risks, staying informed about the organization's direction, and engaging with stakeholders are essential for proactive risk management.

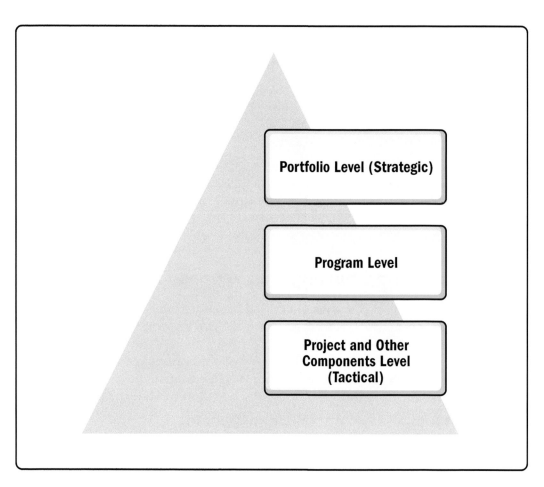

Figure 6-1. Understanding Program Risk Management

6.1.3. Bridging the Risk Management Gaps among the Portfolio, Program, and Project Levels

Risk management plays a critical role in an organization's success, especially when dealing with risks across various levels of portfolios, programs, and projects. Effectively bridging the risk management gaps among these levels can pose significant challenges. By comprehending and proactively addressing these gaps, organizations can strengthen their capacity to navigate uncertainties, optimize resource allocation, and confidently achieve their strategic objectives. The integration of risk management practices across these different levels empowers organizations to make informed decisions, address potential threats, and capitalize on opportunities, ultimately leading to improved overall performance and success.

These risk management practices include:

• **Establishing risk thresholds.** To ensure efficient risk management, it is essential to establish a program risk threshold that determines whether a risk should be managed at the program or project level. This risk threshold is determined based on the level of impact and severity a risk may have. Consistency in assessing risks across different program components is vital. Techniques like expected monetary value (EMV) or risk scores, derived from probability and impact assessments, can be utilized. Another technique to consider is analyzing the program-level schedule impacts of a project-level risk being realized (e.g., a delay in one project resulting in a cascade effect impacting the timelines of multiple other projects in the program). Understanding the risk threshold and maintaining a consistent approach in evaluating risks can be challenging, but is crucial for distinguishing between program-level and project-level risks, based on predefined thresholds. By adhering to these predetermined criteria, program managers can allocate appropriate resources and attention to defined levels of risk, enabling them to address potential issues more effectively and ensure the overall success of the program.

- **Dealing with cumulative risks.** Cumulative risks arise when risks are interconnected or stem from the same source. Managing these risks at the program level is crucial. Breakdown structures, such as risk, work, and organizational breakdown structures, can aid in identifying common categories, groupings, and patterns among risks. By mapping risks against these structures, insights into the relationships among risks can be gained. For instance, risks that impact the same work package, or are related to work packages across programs or projects, can be grouped together. Additionally, risks originating from the same source within the risk breakdown structure can be cumulated. By addressing cumulative risks collectively, program managers can develop more comprehensive and efficient risk response strategies, ensuring that potential impacts are appropriately managed and the overall success of the program is safeguarded.

- **Addressing risks cascading from the portfolio and strategic levels.** Risks emanating from higher levels, such as the board of directors or senior executives, can have substantial repercussions for the portfolio and its associated programs. These strategic and portfolio risks may arise from policy decisions, market positioning, competitive advantage, or portfolio components prioritization. To manage these risks effectively, it is essential to establish a strategy-to-portfolio-to-program risk threshold. This threshold helps in determining when strategic and portfolio risks demand attention at the program level. Clear communication channels and transparent discussions with the board or senior and portfolio managers are vital for effectively addressing these risks. By maintaining open lines of communication, program managers can gain valuable insights into strategic and high-level decisions and their potential impacts on the programs. Proactively managing these risks at the program level ensures better alignment with the organization's strategic vision and enhances the overall chances of success for the entire program.

- **Managing program-level risks.** Program-level risks are unique to the program. It is crucial to openly discuss and address program-level risks to ensure their proper handling and minimize any potential negative impact on the program's success. By proactively managing these risks at the program level, program managers can maintain better control over the program's trajectory, optimize resource allocation, and enhance the program's overall resilience. This comprehensive approach to risk management bolsters the program's chance of achieving its intended objectives and delivering value.

Programs involve a multitude of elements, business-as-usual activities, and related initiatives, leading to distinctive risks that emerge from internal processes, components, and interactions. These risks are shaped by various factors such as the program's structure, scope, stakeholders, resource allocation, and dependencies among program components. It is crucial to identify and address these program-specific risks through the implementation of customized risk assessment, response, and control measures. This implementation involves conducting comprehensive risk assessments, formulating robust risk response strategies, and establishing rigorous risk monitoring and control mechanisms integrated into the program management framework. By diligently addressing these program-level risks, program managers can enhance the program's overall resilience and increase its likelihood of achieving desired outcomes.

Note: Risk level refers to the magnitude of a specific risk event or potential impact on a project or organization. Risk level concentrates on assessing the severity or significance of individual risks, and is often measured in terms of likelihood and impact, helping to prioritize risks based on their potential consequences. Alternatively, a risk profile provides a comprehensive overview of all risks associated with a portfolio, program, project, or organization. A risk profile typically includes information about individual risks, such as their likelihood, impact, response strategies, and overall exposure, to enable stakeholders to understand the overall risk landscape and make informed decisions about risk management priorities and strategies.

6.1.4 Managing Program Overall and Individual Risks

Managing program-level risks necessitates a unique and comprehensive strategy due to their broader scope and complexity. Unlike project-level risk management, addressing program-level risks requires an interconnected approach that considers strategic alignment between the program management plan and organizational strategy, with consideration to the environmental factors found in the environmental assessments. This approach includes defining program risk management goals; identifying, evaluating, and prioritizing risks; conducting quantitative analysis; developing customized responses; implementing risk response strategies; regularly reviewing and updating risk management plans; and maintaining effective communication and reporting practices.

Distinguishing between overall and individual program risk management, alongside the concept of risk efficiency, provides a strategic framework to manage risks within programs. Managing overall risks involves understanding the impact of uncertainties on the entire program and focusing on risk exposure arising from the program's inherent elements such as its structure and scope. Conversely, managing individual risks concentrates on specific uncertain events or conditions that could positively or negatively affect the program's objectives.

Program-level risks are generally classified into escalated risks and cascaded risks. Escalated risks originate from lower levels within the program such as project-based risks, which, when combined, can significantly impact the program. Alternatively, cascaded risks stem from strategic decisions made by higher management or at the portfolio level, which could also affect the program (see Figure 6-2).

To achieve risk efficiency, programs should aim for a balanced group of projects and activities with varied risk-reward profiles. This balancing involves strategically selecting and combining projects with diverse levels of risk to optimize the risk profile and efficiency within the program. Building a risk-efficient program entails carefully evaluating and selecting projects and activities that align with the program's objectives and risk thresholds, and involves considering potential returns, resource allocation, interdependencies, and the impact on strategic goals to create a well-rounded and successful program.

6.1.5 Achieving Flexibility and Resilience in Program Risk Management

Flexibility and resilience are vital to a program's risk management strategy. By designing a program with inherent flexibility, program managers can make necessary adjustments to manage overall risk exposure effectively. Structuring the program into phases enhances resilience, allowing incremental delivery while addressing risks proactively. Program risk management operates at both the overall and individual levels. Both levels are interrelated, influencing each other. A comprehensive strategy, employing standard risk management tools adapted to the program level, strengthens resilience and improves risk management results.

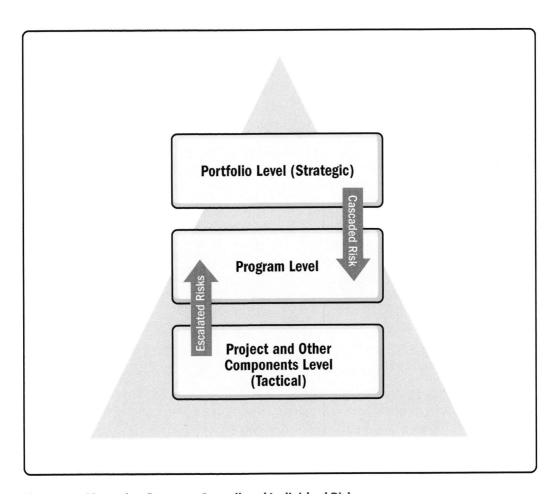

Figure 6-2. Managing Program Overall and Individual Risks

6.1.6 Program Risk Management Implementation Challenges

Implementing program risk management presents several challenges, including but not limited to:

- **Distinguishing between overall and individual risks.** Programs face two types of risks: overall and individual. Managing overall risk exposure requires distinct strategies from those used for handling individual risks, making it essential to address both aspects separately in an effective program risk management plan. For instance, in a program developing a new product line, the overall risk may be related to market demand. Significant changes in market conditions could impact the entire program's success. At the same time, individual risks within the program could include delays in developing specific components due to technical challenges or resource constraints. Similarly, in a program expanding business operations into a new region, the overall risk may be associated with changes in regulatory requirements, affecting multiple projects within the program. At the individual level, one project in the program may face a risk related to securing necessary permits for construction in a specific location. It is also crucial to identify controllable and uncontrollable risks. Controllable risks are those whose causes can be proactively addressed, while uncontrollable risks, like weather conditions, are beyond organizations' control, necessitating planned actions to mitigate their effects. Practitioners often focus solely on dealing with effects, neglecting to address underlying causes. Awareness of controllable risks and the development of proactive action plans to address their causes are key to successful risk management. By recognizing and addressing both overall and individual risks appropriately, program managers can ensure comprehensive risk management and enhance the program's chance of success. It is also important to consider the influence of the uncertainty and ambiguity of the client's requirements, technology innovation and continuous disequilibrium, and the evolving nature of the organization's programs.

- **Building program risk efficiency.** A significant challenge lies in establishing a consistent method for measuring risk and return across the program's projects and components. To ensure meaningful comparison and evaluation of risks, a standard approach is necessary. This approach aims to achieve risk efficiency, which involves optimizing the return for a given level of risk.

- **Identifying the risk baseline.** A risk baseline helps in identifying, documenting, assessing, and managing risks, as it provides a structured framework for understanding and addressing potential challenges and uncertainties throughout the program's life cycle. It represents a snapshot or a point-in-time record of identified risks, their attributes, and their associated information at a specific moment in the program's life cycle. The risk baseline serves several important purposes:

  o **Risk identification.** Risk identification documents all identified risks that could potentially impact the program.

  o **Risk description.** Each risk in the baseline should have a detailed description, including its nature, source, potential consequences, and the factors contributing to its existence.

  o **Risk ownership.** The risk baseline often assigns ownership of each risk to a specific individual or team responsible for responding to and managing each risk. This ownership ensures accountability for addressing and responding to risks.

  o **Risk assessment and prioritization.** Risks in the baseline are typically assessed in terms of their probability (likelihood of occurrence) and impact (severity of consequences). This assessment helps prioritize which risks require the most attention and resources.

  o **Risk response strategies.** The baseline may include initial strategies or plans for managing each risk or other recommendations, especially for cascading risks. These strategies can evolve over time as the program progresses and more information becomes available.

  o **Monitoring and tracking.** The risk baseline serves as a reference point for monitoring changes in risks over time. As the program advances, new risks may emerge, while existing risks may evolve or be dealt with. Changes to the baseline are documented and tracked.

  o **Communication.** The risk baseline provides a means for effective communication among program stakeholders.

  o **Baseline comparison.** The baseline enables comparisons of the current risk baseline to previous versions to assess how the program risk landscape is changing and how risk is escalating from program components. This comparison helps in making informed decisions and adjustments to the risk management strategies.

  o **Risk reporting.** Information from the risk baseline is often included in program status reports to keep stakeholders informed about the state of risk management activities.

Risk baselines and benchmarks play a crucial role in finding the optimal balance between risk and return or impact. By evaluating the potential advantages and disadvantages of high-risk components within the program, program managers can optimize the overall risk exposure while still ensuring that strategic goals are met. This comprehensive approach aids in making informed decisions and achieving the best possible outcomes for the program.

- **Aligning with organizational risk management framework.** Program risk management should be aligned with organizational risk management to account for the organization's unique risk threshold levels and objectives. By considering the organization's specific circumstances and strategic goals, program managers can effectively address risks in a manner that aligns with the broader organizational vision. However, aligning program risk management with organizational risk management poses various challenges. These challenges may include differences in risk cultures, communication and collaboration needs, complexities in process integration, considerations of organizational structure, resource allocation requirements, and efforts related to change management. Overcoming these challenges is vital to ensuring a cohesive and harmonious approach to risk management that enhances the organization's overall resilience and success.

- **Continual program risk monitoring and adjustment.** Achieving risk efficiency is an iterative and continuous process that demands constant monitoring of risks throughout the program life cycle. The process involves identifying, assessing, and responding to risks in a manner that adapts to the program's evolution and external changes. Regular reassessment ensures that risk management strategies remain aligned with the program's current state and environment—accommodating new risks, changes in known risks, or the retirement of irrelevant risks. Based on these reassessments, adjustments are made, such as revising response plans, reallocating resources, or updating the program's risk profile. This ongoing process maintains an optimal risk-return balance, bolstering the program's resilience, flexibility, and likelihood of achieving its objectives amid the ever-changing landscape of risks and uncertainties. Continuous monitoring and adaptation are essential to equip the program to navigate challenges and seize opportunities throughout its life cycle. By staying proactive and responsive, the program can effectively manage risks, ensuring that it remains on track to meet its strategic goals. This dynamic approach to risk management maximizes the program's ability to succeed in a constantly evolving environment, enhancing its overall performance and outcomes.

- **Tailoring risk management approaches.** Managing risks at the program level requires a strategic mindset, where program managers should grasp the program's strategic objectives and broader context. This shift involves moving away from a focus solely on project deliverables and constraints to instead aligning actions with organizational objectives to address higher-level risks. It is crucial to consider factors such as the overall program strategy, stakeholder alignment, and long-term benefits. Additionally, different program types, such as strategic, operational, and compliance programs, come with their own unique characteristics and risk considerations. As a result, risk management approaches should be tailored to each program type's distinct risk exposures. Taking this holistic view ensures a robust risk management framework that integrates strategic objectives with tailored, program-specific considerations, leading to more effective risk management and successful program outcomes.

- **Risk management integration.** Integrating risk management into the overall program management is of the utmost importance. This integration involves coordinating and communicating among risk management and other program management functions to ensure a cohesive approach. Making risk-informed decisions is vital for effective program management, and implementing a continuous monitoring and evaluation process helps in staying proactive.

At the program level, risks encompass both project-specific risks and risks associated with other program components that demand attention and proper responses at this level. Furthermore, it is essential to incorporate risks stemming from strategic and portfolio-level changes and program-level interface risks into the risk management process. Considering all these aspects creates a comprehensive program risk management framework that enhances the program's resilience and contributes to achieving its objectives.

6.2 Program Risk Management Life Cycle

The risk management life cycle, as described in Section 4, is generally applicable to program management. However, there are several additional considerations specific to the program management context that should be taken into account.

6.2.1 Program Risk Identification

Risk identification at the program level focuses on identifying the risks that could impact the delivery of expected benefits. It also focuses on the organization's ability to take over and use the results of the components that are part of the program's scope.

There are three levels where risks relevant to the program can be identified:

- Risks cascading from the portfolio or enterprise level that can affect the achievement of program objectives;

- Risks identified directly at the program level and triggered by program activities, their interdependencies, and activities related to the integration of the components' results to generate the expected benefits; and

- Risks escalated from the program components.

Case Study: Program Management in the Context of the Compact Wind Turbine Project

Based on the case study of the municipality's green portfolio, we can identify several program-level risks that are associated with the energy program, the public safety program, and the carbon data app project, which is a component in the portfolio that interacts with other programs and components. These risks arise directly from program activities, their interdependencies, and the integration of various components to deliver expected benefits.

Some case study examples where risks may cascade down from the green portfolio or overall municipal level and could affect achieving the program's objectives include:

- **Interdependency risk.** The Compact Wind Turbine Project is interconnected with other projects within the energy program. If there is a delay or failure in any of these interconnected projects, it may jeopardize the timely completion and success of the entire program. For instance, a delay in procuring materials for the wind turbines can impact the construction timeline, and thus, the overall program schedule.

- **Benefit realization risk.** The public safety program aims to enhance safety and security. If the implemented measures do not effectively reduce accidents associated with the green portfolio, or if they are not accepted or used correctly by the public, the expected benefits of the program will not be realized. This is a risk tied directly to program activities and their desired outcomes. In this case, the benefit realization risk from the public safety program could be escalated to the portfolio level. Materialization of this risk necessitates program completion and closure of program-level risks. Upon escalation, the portfolio manager becomes responsible for its management, potentially initiating mitigating actions to be implemented by the program manager. This underscores a strategic shift from managing program-specific risks to addressing broader, portfolio-wide concerns.

- **Cross-program risk.** There is a risk that the energy generated by the Compact Wind Turbine Project may not meet the power needs of the public safety program or other programs or portfolios within the municipality, jeopardizing its operations. This risk is tied to the interdependency of results from different programs within the portfolio.

The program risks are identified from their operational and contextual perspectives:

- **Operational risks.** Risks at the operational level are directly triggered by program activities such as integration of the results of projects and their related transition, change management, and triggering of operational activities. In addition, some operational risks may result from the escalation of the components' risks when these risks have an impact that expands beyond the perimeter of accountability of the component managers or their specific budgets. For example, the portfolio's stand-alone carbon data app project aims to monitor and manage the municipality's carbon footprint. If the data from the energy program (like the wind turbine energy production) and the public safety program (like the carbon footprint of security infrastructure) are not accurately integrated into the app within the proper timeframe, it may lead to incorrect carbon footprint calculations, thereby not achieving the expected benefit of effective carbon management. This risk could be identified within the mentioned programs as a risk triggered by program activities.

- **Contextual risks.** Contextual risks are those risks resulting from the strategic and organizational environment of the program, including the stakeholders, variations in the strategy, or the evolution of the business environment or program's business case. Some contextual risks may also be escalated from the program components when their impact and treatment exceed the boundary of accountability of the components' managers.

Referring to the case study, risks related to stakeholder engagement can be identified as follows: The diverse stakeholder group is vital in managing project risks and driving the green portfolio toward its ultimate strategic objective. However, misalignment or conflicts of interest among stakeholders, such as environmental assessment advocates opposing certain aspects of the wind turbine project or local community members resisting public safety measures, can pose significant risks at the program level, affecting the realization of program benefits.

Some risks identified at the program level or escalated from the project level may need to be escalated to the enterprise or portfolio level. These risks impact the business and operational performance generated through the exploitation of the business capabilities created by the program. Escalated risks follow the same analysis processes as other risks identified at the program level.

6.2.2 Program Risk Qualitative and Quantitative Analyses

Evaluation of risks at the program level is performed by considering the depth of each risk's impact on the realization of the expected benefits or the development of the expected organizational capability. The aim of these analyses is to evaluate whether or not the impact can be contained within the limits of the program budget, timelines, and other success criteria.

When the impact affects the program's ability to deliver its benefits or organizational capabilities, then the risk is addressed at the program level.

When the impact affects the ability of the organization to deliver the performance and value expected to be obtained from the benefits and capabilities created by the program, then the risk and its treatment are escalated to the enterprise or portfolio level. In addition, the risk and its treatment are escalated when the risk affects the expected financial and operational performance anticipated from the new capabilities beyond the agreed thresholds.

Case Study: Program Risk Analyses in the Compact Wind Turbine Project

The following are some examples of how qualitative and quantitative analyses could be used in the municipality case study. These examples note that risk treatment would require balancing cost, schedule, and the ability to deliver expected benefits and organizational capabilities. If impacts exceed the agreed thresholds, risks should be escalated to higher levels for more resources or strategic decision-making:

- **Energy program—interdependency risk (qualitative and quantitative analysis).** The risk that a delay in an interconnected project will impact the Compact Wind Turbine Project can be evaluated qualitatively by discussing with project managers and assessing the likelihood and impact based on previous similar projects. Quantitatively, we can model the potential time delay and calculate its cost implications. If the impact can be contained within the program budget and timelines, it is managed at the program level. But if this delay threatens the entire program's ability to deliver its benefits (e.g., energy production falls below necessary levels for the municipality), the risk should be escalated to the portfolio or enterprise level.

- **Public safety program—benefits realization risk (qualitative analysis).** This risk can be assessed qualitatively by soliciting feedback from the public and law enforcement officials. If the public safety measures do not effectively reduce safety concerns or are not well received by the community, this could prevent the realization of program benefits. This risk could be addressed at the program level through community outreach or revisions to the measures. But if the risk affects the municipality's overall ability to ensure public safety, it may need to be escalated to the portfolio level.

- **Carbon data app project—integration risk (quantitative analysis).** This risk can be assessed quantitatively by performing data accuracy checks and system integration tests. If the integration errors are minor and can be corrected within the project budget, this risk is addressed at the project level. However, if major errors could undermine the entire program's ability to monitor and manage the municipality's carbon footprint effectively, this risk would escalate to the program, portfolio, or enterprise level.

- **Cross-program risk (qualitative and quantitative analysis).** If the Compact Wind Turbine Project cannot meet the energy needs of the public safety program, this could affect both programs. The risk can be assessed qualitatively by discussions with the project teams, and quantitatively by analyzing the energy demands and generation capacities. The risk would be handled at the program level if the shortfall can be compensated within the budget (e.g., through energy-saving measures or purchasing additional power). If not, the risk would need to be escalated.

- **Risk related to stakeholder engagement (qualitative analysis).** This risk can be assessed qualitatively by engaging stakeholders, understanding their concerns, and evaluating the potential impact on the project outcomes. If stakeholder disagreements can be managed within the program through negotiation or compromise, they can be handled at the program level. If the conflicts threaten the municipality's sustainability and energy independence goals, the risk would be escalated to the portfolio or enterprise level.

6.2.3 Program Risk Response Strategies

In principle, all potential responses listed in Section 4 may be used when responding to risks at the program level.

Strategies developed to deal with risks at the program level consist of the activities agreed upon in the risk management plan and budgeted for in the program's budget or contingency reserve. Some of the responses are also developed due to escalation from the component level. These risk responses consist of adding program activities or components, updating the program baselines, or removing components from the program.

These new components are intended to maximize the creation of further business benefits or enhance organizational capabilities development. Alternatively, the intent may be to maintain or reinforce the program's contribution to achieve related strategic objectives or minimize threats to the organization's objectives and strategy.

Case Study: Program Risk Response Strategies in the Compact Wind Turbine Project

The following strategies are designed to respond to the previously identified risks in the case study. The main aim of these strategies would be to either enhance the program's ability to create or realize benefits and develop organizational capabilities, or to minimize threats to the program and the municipality's strategic objectives. These strategies should be documented in the risk management plan and adequately budgeted for in the program's budget or contingency reserve, and then addressed where applicable with schedule buffers and other contingency measures.

Some potential risk categories and response strategies at the program level:

- **Energy program—interdependency risk.** A contingency plan can be developed and budgeted to manage unexpected delays or issues in interconnected projects. This plan may include having backup suppliers or additional resources on standby. Also, additional project management oversight could be added to the program to ensure better coordination and early detection of potential delays or issues.

- **Public safety program—benefit realization risk.** The program could introduce new components like community outreach initiatives, training sessions, or public awareness campaigns to enhance public acceptance and efficacy of safety measures. These components would be designed to maximize the program's benefits by ensuring the measures are used correctly and accepted by the community.

- **Carbon data app project—integration risk.** An additional component, like a dedicated data integration team or a third-party data auditing service, could be added to the program. This approach would aim to enhance the project's capability to integrate data accurately, and thus, effectively manage the municipality's carbon footprint.

- **Cross-program risk.** The energy program could add a new project or initiative focused on energy efficiency or backup power sources to ensure the energy demands of the public safety program are met. This approach could involve updating the program baselines to account for these new initiatives. The costs of such an initiative would need to be weighed against the expected costs of realization of this cross-program risk.

- **Risk related to stakeholder engagement.** A proactive stakeholder engagement plan could be developed and included in the program. This plan could feature regular meetings, transparent communication, and dispute-resolution processes. The intent would be to maintain the program's alignment with the strategic objectives by minimizing potential stakeholder conflicts.

6.2.4 Implementing Program Risk Responses

Implementation of risk responses within a program consists of:

- Triggering the risk responses as they have been defined in the risk management plan,

- Transferring the corresponding budget from the reserves into the budget at completion,

- Dropping one high-risk project to protect the whole program's benefits, and

- Updating the program baselines accordingly.

When new components are added, they become part of the regular program scope and are subject to the application of the standard program delivery and deployment processes.

Implementation of risk responses at the component level is aligned and performed in coordination with the responses that are implemented at the program level. Any formally approved risk response is integral to the program management plan. Implementing an approved risk response is not a change to the program initiated through a formal, integrated program change management procedure. However, any new responses planned to address emergent risks that could affect program baselines would become part of the integrated program change management procedure.

6.2.5 Monitoring Program Risks

Monitoring risks at the program level is both a tactical and strategic activity:

- **Tactical activity.** Tactical activities oversee the aspects related to the execution of the anticipatory and responsive actions undertaken to respond to identified risks and the ongoing identification, analysis, and response to new risks.

- **Strategic activity.** Strategic activities address the evolution of the risk characteristics of each program component individually, the overall program's risk profile, and the impact of that evolution on the business benefits or organizational capabilities it is intended to generate.

Case Study: Monitoring Program Risks in the Compact Wind Turbine Project

In the Compact Wind Turbine Project, monitoring program risks as a tactical activity within the energy program includes assessing the effectiveness of contingency plans for unexpected project delays (e.g., backup suppliers, additional resources), which could be monitored by tracking project timelines, costs, and deliverables' quality. For the public safety program, the effectiveness of community outreach initiatives could be monitored by tracking public sentiment, crime rates, and usage rates of safety measures.

Monitoring program risks as a strategic activity in the Compact Wind Turbine Project could include regular risk assessments that can be conducted for each component of both the energy program and public safety program, looking at changes in risk factors like material availability, weather conditions, community acceptance, regulatory changes, etc. The carbon data app project's risk profile can be analyzed in terms of data accuracy, integration success, and user adoption rates. Monitoring how these risk profiles evolve helps identify new risks or inefficiencies in the response strategies, which may affect the realization of expected benefits or the development of organizational capabilities.

These risk profiles are regularly analyzed in order to identify any potential trends that indicate new risks or the inefficiency or ineffectiveness of the response strategies.

The monitoring of risk responses is conducted according to their quantitative and qualitative parameters, as defined in the management plans, considering the overall impact from the component to the enterprise level. For example, in the case of stakeholder engagement risk, the effectiveness of the stakeholder engagement plan could be assessed qualitatively by the quality of stakeholder interactions and conflict resolution outcomes. Stakeholder feedback, meeting attendance, or resolution time could be tracked quantitatively.

These risk responses are intended to effectively treat the respective specific risks and contribute to enhancing or maintaining the realization of expected benefits. It is important to perform a qualitative assessment to ensure that the risk responses are efficient and effective.

Monitoring risks at the program level also includes ensuring that risk-related elements of the governance framework are properly implemented by the program's component managers and that they are effective.

6.3 Integration of Risk Management into the Program Management Performance Domains

Several risk management practices can be applied across the program life cycle within all of the performance domains to achieve their objectives (see Figure 6-3). These practices typically cover the areas shown in Table 6-1.

6.3.1 Strategic Alignment

Strategic Alignment ensures that a program contributes to organizational strategy in the expected way. Risk management efforts at the program level address new strategic opportunities and threats. When necessary, these efforts lead to appropriate program redefinition or changes in the relevant program components.

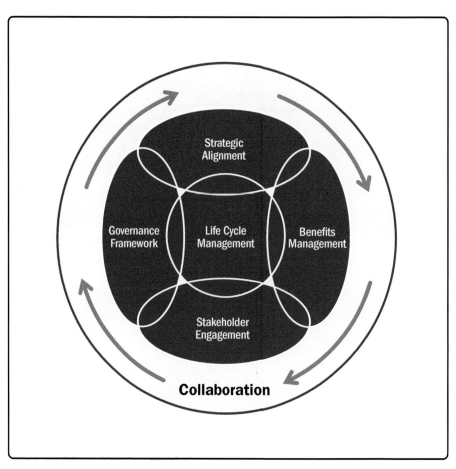

Figure 6-3. Program Management Performance Domains (Source: *The Standard for Program Management* [4])

6.3.2 Benefits Management

Benefits Management ensures that the program benefits described in the business case and other program governance documents are successfully realized. The main focus of risk management in this area is to (a) identify opportunities that could increase these benefits, (b) take advantage of opportunities more efficiently and effectively, and (c) manage threats that could potentially jeopardize the program's efforts to realize its benefits.

6.3.3 Stakeholder Engagement

From the program perspective, key stakeholders typically include program governance board members, the program manager, managers of program components, partners, key suppliers, and regulators impacting or being impacted by the program benefits. From this perspective, program risk management focuses on opportunities for increasing effectiveness in realizing program benefits and on minimizing threats that could lower the ability to do so. It is realized by effective engagement of stakeholders at the program level and ensures consistency of stakeholder engagement strategies among program components.

Table 6-1. Areas of the Program Management Performance Domains Typically Covered by Risk Management Practices

Performance Domain	Areas Covered by Risk Management Practices
Strategic Alignment	• Program business case • Program risk management approach • Environmental assessments
Benefits Management	• Program objectives • Opportunities for new benefits • Efficiency and effectiveness of benefits realization • Sustainability of program benefits
Stakeholder Engagement	• Methods for stakeholder identification, categorization, and analysis • Attitude of key program stakeholders • Interactions and conflicts of interests • Ways of engaging stakeholders • Scope, channels, techniques, and frequency of communications
Governance Framework	• Program governance structures, policies, and procedures • Assignment of individuals to key governance roles • Program complexity • Risk escalation policies • Effectiveness of risk management
Collaboration	• Value delivery planning • Program alignment • Program complexity
Life Cycle Management	• Program definition phase activities • Component authorization and planning • Component oversight and integration • Component transition

6.3.4 Governance Framework

The Governance Framework performance domain uses the framework, functions, and processes by which a program is monitored, managed, and supported in order to meet organizational strategic and operational goals. The governance framework also addresses program complexity in an effort to reduce it. These activities are backed by risk management practices and focused on analyzing various governance approaches from the risk perspective. In addition, the selection of individuals to perform key governance roles is supported by risk analysis.

From the risk management perspective, a key element of the governance framework is the risk escalation process, which is integrated with processes within components and backed by program governance processes and structures.

6.3.5 Collaboration

Collaboration is interwoven throughout all aspects of program management. Risk management is an inherent part of the Collaboration performance domain supporting the optimization of programs for benefits delivery.

6.3.6 Life Cycle Management

The Life Cycle Management performance domain ensures that program definition, delivery, and closure activities are effectively managed. This is accomplished to ensure program benefits are realized using the right set of components, in the right sequence, and with adherence to the program's business case and other governance documents.

Risk management in this area focuses on identifying and addressing program-level risks as early as possible. This is achieved by fully integrating risk identification, analysis, and response planning throughout all program and component activities.

Case Study: Program Management Performance Domains in the Compact Wind Turbine Project

Strategic Alignment in the Compact Wind Turbine Project

Strategic Alignment in the municipality's green portfolio context ensures that the programs contribute to the organization's strategy as intended as follows:

- **Strategic opportunities.** New developments, such as advancements in renewable energy technology or rising public interest in carbon tracking, could present opportunities to enhance the programs' contributions to the strategic objectives.

- **Strategic threats.** Potential threats, like changing regulations or rising crime rates, could jeopardize the programs' alignment with the strategic objectives.

- **Risk responses.** Risk management identifies and responds to these opportunities and threats, possibly leading to program changes. For example, the energy program may adopt new technology, the public safety program may introduce new safety measures, and the carbon data app project may enhance its data security. Maintaining this alignment as the strategic landscape evolves ensures that the programs continue to support the strategic objectives of sustainability and carbon neutrality.

Benefits Management in the Compact Wind Turbine Project

In the case study, Benefits Management ensures that the benefits of each program in the municipality's green portfolio are realized as follows:

- **Energy program.** Opportunities may include exploring new renewable technologies or securing grants to increase benefits. Efficient delivery could involve optimizing timelines or supplier reliability. Threats may result from design inconsistencies or regulatory changes.

- **Public safety program.** Opportunities could be partnerships with community organizations or new technologies. Efficiency may be improved by training local personnel or using data analytics. Threats could be public resistance or unexpected crime rate increases.

- **Carbon data app project.** Opportunities could include integration with other systems or public access. Efficiency may be improved through agile development or automated testing. Threats may include technological failures or data breaches.

Stakeholder Engagement in the Compact Wind Turbine Project

For example, by engaging stakeholders effectively, the municipality can maximize the realization of program benefits and minimize threats. For instance, consistent engagement with developers, data providers, and users could uncover opportunities to improve the carbon data app's functionality and user experience, thus increasing its benefits. Furthermore, coordination with cybersecurity experts could help mitigate potential threats of data breaches.

Governance Framework in the Compact Wind Turbine Project

For the municipality's green portfolio, the Governance Framework performance domain considerations may involve the following:

- **Governance framework.** This element involves establishing a governance framework for each program, such as the energy program, public safety program, and carbon data app project. The framework defines roles, responsibilities, decision-making processes, reporting structures, and risk escalation pathways, providing a structured approach to managing program-level complexities.

- **Risk management integration.** This element involves incorporating risk management practices into governance approaches. For instance, the governance board may regularly review risk analyses to understand potential threats and opportunities. This would inform decision-making processes, helping to mitigate risks and capitalize on opportunities, which may involve adjusting project timelines, reallocating resources, or changing strategic approaches.

- **Key governance roles.** This element involves leveraging risk analysis to select individuals for key governance roles. For example, an individual with extensive experience in managing regulatory compliance may be chosen to oversee the Compact Wind Turbine Project due to its regulatory risks.

- **Risk escalation process.** Implementing a risk escalation process allows for the seamless transfer of risk management from the component to the program level. If a risk cannot be effectively managed within a project, such as a significant cost overrun in the Compact Wind Turbine Project, it would be escalated to the program governance board.

Collaboration in the Compact Wind Turbine Project

In the case study, Collaboration is interwoven throughout all aspects of the municipality's program management, taking value delivery planning, program alignment, and program complexity into consideration. Risk management, as an inherent part of the Collaboration performance domain, supports the optimization of the municipality's programs to help ensure the delivery of benefits overall.

Life Cycle Management in the Compact Wind Turbine Project

Life Cycle Management in the municipality's green portfolio ensures that each program, from the energy program to the public safety program, is effectively managed from definition to delivery and closure. Risks such as cost overruns, regulatory challenges, public resistance, or technological failures are identified, analyzed, and addressed proactively throughout the program life cycle. This approach, integrated into every stage of the program, ensures the timely realization of program benefits in line with the business case and governance documents while mitigating potential risks.

6.3.7 Program Activities

Even though the management of program-level activities often differs significantly from the component level, risk management processes for the supporting program activities are similar in nature to the component projects.

The governance framework establishes policies on risk management among the program and its components, including escalation mechanisms. These policies help ensure that there are no gaps among the component and program levels that are not covered by risk management practices.

Case Study: Program Activities in the Compact Wind Turbine Project

In the municipality's green portfolio, program activities are designed to ensure smooth program execution. For instance, if a risk arises, like a significant cost overrun in one project, it would be escalated to the program level. This integration ensures no gaps exist in risk management coverage among the program and its components.

7

Risk Management in the Context of Project Management

The purpose of risk management at the project level is to support the optimal delivery of project results, leading to the realization of the benefits for which the project was undertaken. In addition, risk management helps to ensure this occurs within the identified project constraints.

Projects aim to create a unique product, service, or result, with their success gauged by the ability to meet defined objectives and deliver value. Uncertainties from operational activities and enterprise environmental factors (EEFs) introduce risks. These risks, evaluated based on their potential impact on achieving project objectives and value, are primarily assessed at the tactical level. While the broader considerations related to expected value or benefits are often elevated to the portfolio or program governance level, it is vital to understand that expected value analysis also takes place at the project level. Ensuring that project teams are aligned with the strategic objectives that initiated the project's authorization is paramount, as this empowers them to proactively manage both opportunities and threats. It is worth noting that a project's authorization is not solely for risk management; it is for the entirety of project activities, with risk management being a pivotal component.

7.1 Risk Management Gaps among the Project and Higher Levels

As described in previous sections, risk management is critical to an organization's success, particularly when managing risks across different levels of portfolios, programs, projects, and organizational structures. However, specific factors should be considered and communicated to the appropriate stakeholders when addressing risks at the project level.

Since not all organizations have formal risk management structures, it can be challenging to find support for projects. In such cases, integrating risk management into project processes becomes crucial, along with fostering cross-functional communication about potential risks and seeking advice from internal experts or external consultants. Educating employees on risk management principles and continuously learning from past projects to refine practices are also essential strategies for effectively managing risks in organizations without formal structures such as a project management office or enterprise risk management.

7.1.1 Establishing Risk Thresholds

Risk thresholds should be defined in order to evaluate if a risk can be managed at the project level or should be escalated to higher levels for further action. A project team should engage with stakeholders to understand their risk appetites and risk thresholds. A qualitative method should be used to define risk thresholds and can be guided by the expected monetary value (EMV) or the probability and impact defined in the project risk matrix. The risks that are within the risk appetite can be managed by the project manager at the project level. However, the risks outside of the risk appetite should be escalated to higher levels. Thresholds should be captured in the project's risk management plan and are typically stated and communicated to the project team and reflected in the definition of risk impact levels for the project. Various risk response strategies can be implemented in either of the mentioned scenarios. It is crucial to reinforce consistency through structured risk management governance.

The risk threshold, which represents the level of risk a project can tolerate, is a crucial factor in deciding whether to escalate a risk to higher decision levels. Ignoring the risk threshold can lead to inefficient resource allocation and may cause practitioners to overlook risks that genuinely require higher-level attention.

7.1.2 Addressing Risks from Higher and Strategic Levels

Organizational and high-level portfolio and program risks can significantly impact the risks of the project. Enterprise environmental factors, such as strategic decisions, enterprise resource management, market positioning, competitive advantages in the market, and strategic objectives, can affect the viability of a project. As described in Section 4, a decision to implement a project can be a response to reduce the portfolio risks or exploit the opportunities within the organization. These goals and objectives are achieved, in part, by aligning responsibility and accountability for risk management with the organizational business model.

7.1.3 Project-Level Risk Interfaces with Operations

In the broader context, projects interact with various operational aspects within the organization. To ensure smooth operations, it is crucial to effectively manage the potential risks that may affect both the project and its interfaces with operations.

It is equally important to capitalize on project-level opportunities that can foster improved coordination with operations. This involves optimizing resource allocation, cutting costs, enhancing efficiency, and bolstering reliability at the higher management levels. Organizations should establish a shared understanding of risk and be well prepared to address both anticipated threats and opportunities.

Additionally, it is critical to identify the various organizational levels that the project may interact with, which include not only executive management, but also operations management, portfolio management, program components, and project teams. It is worth noting that there are different organizational structures, not just projectized structures. In matrix or functional organizations, for example, projects are intertwined with the wider organizational framework, rather than operating as isolated entities.

7.2 Project Risk Management Life Cycle

The life cycle of risk management, as described in Section 4, generally applies to project management. However, there are several additional considerations for the corresponding processes that should be taken into account in this context.

Various techniques can be used for project risk management life cycle processes, which are listed throughout this section.

7.2.1 Enhancing Risk Analysis and Involving the Right Participants

When it comes to conducting a comprehensive risk analysis, it is essential to assemble the appropriate individuals. The project charter and initial planning teams can serve as a foundation for more extensive and iterative risk analysis sessions.

Once the project is underway and in the execution phase, these team members, serving as subject matter experts, contribute critical perspectives that are indispensable for an in-depth risk analysis. They offer insights that may not be readily available to the project manager.

Hence, the inclusion of team members in the risk analysis process is of paramount importance. The time allocated to risk assessment and analysis sessions may vary depending on the project management approach (adaptive, predictive, or hybrid), as well as other factors such as the project's size and complexity.

Case Study: Project Management in the Context of the Compact Wind Turbine Project

In reference to the case study that is used throughout this practice guide, the involvement of cross-functional teams is imperative to ensuring effective risk analysis. These teams should encompass a range of knowledge, skills, and expertise, including technical proficiency, domain or business acumen, financial prowess, and regulatory compliance competence. This collaborative composition is important to the comprehensive assessment of risks.

Engaging local community members, recognized as other key stakeholders, is also crucial. Their perspectives on social and environmental impacts, as well as their concerns, should be incorporated into risk assessments. For example, they may articulate concerns related to noise pollution or the aesthetic implications of wind turbines.

In addition, media representatives should be actively engaged to transparently communicate risk management efforts to the public. Effective media interaction can significantly influence public perceptions and expectations regarding the project's inherent risks.

Conducting regular stakeholder meetings is fundamental. These meetings facilitate open discussions on project progress and risks, cultivating a sense of shared responsibility and collaboration among stakeholders, thus ensuring their active participation in risk management efforts.

Moreover, agricultural landowners, particularly those hosting turbines, should be included in risk discussions regarding land use agreements, potential impacts on farming activities, and compensation arrangements in the event of adverse effects.

In certain scenarios, the involvement of external experts or consultants, possessing specialized knowledge in wind turbine technology, environmental impact assessments, or regulatory compliance, can be advantageous. These experts offer objective insights into potential risks, further fortifying the project's risk assessment process.

7.2.2 Project Risk Identification

Identification of risks at the project level is based on operational and contextual inputs. Operational inputs come from the activities of the project itself. Among these inputs are:

- **Project scope statement.** There are several risks related to the specifications and agreed-upon methods of delivery for products, services, or other results that are expected to be delivered by the project.

- **Project management approach.** Regardless of the approach selected, the approach itself introduces some risks to the project. The adaptive, predictive, and hybrid project approaches have different levels of risks and uncertainty, as described in Section 4.

- **Work breakdown structure (WBS), activity list, or backlog.** There are some risks directly connected to the decomposition of the project work and triggered by its execution.

- **Estimates.** Estimates are performed in terms of time, cost, effort, resources, and velocity. The target accuracy of an estimate is the level of risk tolerated.

- **Dependencies and sequence of work.** Interdependencies and the resulting sequence of work are sources of risk. In predictive approaches, special attention should be paid to the critical path and external dependencies created by the sharing of resources with other projects. If the critical path changes during the project life cycle, the criticality of the risks related to the elements on that critical path may also be dynamic. Alternatively, in adaptive approaches, in the backlog, the use of feedback, interdependencies of epics, and user stories should be carefully considered.

- **Procurement plans.** Subcontracting parts of the project scope may involve risk transfer, which may also trigger new risks or secondary risks.

- **Change requests.** Each time a change is implemented within a project, it may eliminate certain risks but may also trigger new ones. The potential risks (threats or opportunities) resulting from implementing the change request should be identified and managed throughout the project life cycle, whether applying an adaptive, predictive, or hybrid project management approach.

- **Historical data.** Based on experience, it is important to identify systemic risks and expedite their treatment. Systemic risks are identified at the portfolio level and should be managed across all of the projects within the portfolio.

Contextual risks result from the consideration of enterprise environmental factors (EEFs), organizational process assets (OPAs), and other strategic or organizational aspects shaping the environment of the project such as:

- **Organizational process assets (OPAs).** Standard operating procedures, templates, or organizational policies may be too stringent and rigid, or they may require extended approval chains that can result in project delays or cost escalations. Also, the negotiation process may not allow for any accommodations from the contractors, resulting in constrained relationships.

- **Stakeholder analysis.** Key stakeholders can bring several opportunities to be exploited; however, when handled inadequately, they may introduce threats that should be addressed.

- **Business case.** The business case often implies a factor of profitability or positive return on investment that is exposed to a certain level of uncertainty or risk. The ability to achieve and sustain benefits after project completion is part of risk identification. Risks impacting the realization of benefits can be addressed during project execution.

- **Program- or portfolio-governance-level success factors.** These factors may vary over time and change the priority level of the project within the program or portfolio.

- **Enterprise environmental factors (EEFs).** Factors such as the strategy of the organization, its structure, the dynamics of its business environment, or the variability of its regulatory environment can be triggers of risks that directly impact the project.

Case Study: Project Risk Identification in the Compact Wind Turbine Project

Operational Input Risks in the Compact Wind Turbine Project

- **Project scope statement.** In the municipality, preferential engineering is a risk to the Compact Wind Turbine Project. This risk involves additional considerations and features to the project scope to satisfy all of the stakeholders, rather than the agreed-upon project scope. The potential consequences may be cost overruns and delays to the project.

- **Project management approach.** The Compact Wind Turbine Project is being implemented using a predictive life cycle. However, the carbon data app is being managed iteratively using a hybrid life cycle. The risk management structure, reviews, flexibility, adaptivity, transparency, and communication are varied within the green portfolio, raising the potential for risks related to the project management approach.

- **Work breakdown structure (WBS), activity list, or backlog.** There are also key considerations when creating the WBS and activity list from the business case development used for the delivery schedule of the Compact Wind Turbine Project, such as hierarchy levels, integration of subsystems, standardization, sequence of activities, or duration estimation.

- **Estimates.** The municipality used specific software for the estimation of the cost of the projects based on their nature. For the Compact Wind Turbine Project, the target accuracy was achieved by incorporating the complexity and qualitative risk ratings with specific values based on the industry standards.

- **Dependencies and sequence of work.** Referring to the green portfolio, the interdependencies within the public safety program and the carbon data app project have a potential impact on the timeframe and cost of the Compact Wind Turbine Project. For instance, at a point in time during the delivery phase, additional resources may be required to compress the wind turbine schedule to fulfill the interdependencies with other projects. As a result, the schedule risk may increase and additional costs may be incurred.

- **Procurement plans.** Supply chain disruptions may be another risk for the Compact Wind Turbine Project. Potential consequences of this risk could be project delays, cost overruns, and reputational impacts to the municipality.

- **Change requests.** A recent change request was approved by the municipality to mitigate the delays to the project schedule as a result of procurement complexities. Though this change mitigates one risk, it introduces new risks related to the availability of resources and increased project costs.

- **Historical data.** A lack of qualified design resources in the energy market poses a risk to the Compact Wind Turbine Project. The municipality has raised it as a systemic risk to higher management levels and the boards of directors from past projects. Potential proactive measures may include utilizing a design and construction (D&C) contract type or early engagement of the planning partners.

(Continued)

Contextual Input Risks in the Compact Wind Turbine Project

- **Organizational process assets (OPAs).** Due to the complexity and public-facing nature of the Compact Wind Turbine Project, there are many procedures, templates, and policies that should be followed by the municipality, some of which require lengthy approval processes. These processes can delay the project schedule or cause cost escalations.

- **Stakeholder analysis.** Several stakeholders, who are either internal or external, have been identified for the Compact Wind Turbine Project. For example, a failure to engage with customers and the community is a reputational risk to the municipality, which should be addressed early in the planning phase.

- **Business case.** A key risk in the context of the Compact Wind Turbine Project is the failure to consider the constructability of the wind turbine in the business case development and option engineering. This risk could impact the construction and benefits realization later in the delivery.

- **Program- or portfolio-governance-level success factors.** The Compact Wind Turbine Project may not have been funded due to escalations in the market. So, the municipality could have decided to define another project within the green portfolio or to hold this project for a certain period.

- **Enterprise environmental factors (EEFs).** Environmental regulations may impact the necessity of implementing the Compact Wind Turbine Project or may increase its compliance risk.

7.2.3 Project Risk Qualitative and Quantitative Analyses

The evaluation of risks at the project level is performed by taking into account the degree of impact on the project objectives and the probability of occurrence. The purpose of these analyses is to evaluate whether or not the impact can be contained within the limits of the project budget and the boundary of accountability of the project manager. Risks that have an impact evaluated as containable within the limits of accountability of the project manager and team are dealt with in the project risk management plan and strategy. Every risk impact that exceeds the limits of accountability is escalated to the appropriate governance level.

If the risk impacts the ability of the organization to obtain or sustain the expected benefits, then the risk and its treatment are escalated to the appropriate governance level.

Case Study: Project Risk Analyses in the Compact Wind Turbine Project

In the case study, the Compact Wind Turbine Project core team identified the risk associated with interdependencies between the public safety program and the carbon data app project as high risk, exceeding the project's risk threshold. The wind turbine's project manager, with restricted accountability for the project, took the initiative to escalate this risk to the portfolio manager. In response, the portfolio manager decided to address this risk by proactively coordinating among the interdependent projects, thus mitigating the potential negative impacts.

7.2.4 Project Risk Response Strategies

In principle, all of the potential responses listed in Section 4 can be used when responding to risks at the project level.

The strategies developed to deal with risks at the project level consist of activities that are guided by the risk management plan, budgeted for accordingly, and funded by the project's contingency reserve. Risk responses consist of additional activities or work packages to update the project's baselines or remove activities from these same baselines.

Whenever the project is part of a program or managed as part of a portfolio, escalation of risks to a higher governance level is always one of the available responses. Escalation can increase the effectiveness or efficiency of dealing with specific risks impacting the program or portfolio, or with risks requiring funding above the project's contingency reserves.

Seeking decisions from upper management levels (program or portfolio) regarding go/no-go determinations for specific project scope elements or the project as a whole is essential. The heightened risks that transcend individual project authority often necessitate interactions that may recommend project cancellation or the trimming of chartered scope elements and project objectives.

Case Study: Project Risk Response Strategies in the Compact Wind Turbine Project

In the case study, when a risk materializes and gets escalated to the higher level, the program or portfolio manager will have the authority to transfer the contingencies to the project budget. Then, the project manager should update the project scope and time baselines to reflect the risk response impacts.

7.2.5 Implementing Project Risk Responses

The implementation of risk responses within a project is performed according to the risk management plan, uses the corresponding budget from the reserves into the budget, and updates the project baselines accordingly. Together, these activities become part of the regular project scope and are subject to the application of project execution processes.

Case Study: Implementing Project Risk Responses in the Compact Wind Turbine Project

For instance, in the case study, a community and stakeholder engagement plan is developed to identify and manage the expectations of the local community of the Compact Wind Turbine Project. Also, a community review group is formed to engage the community during the project life cycle.

In some scenarios, the implementation of a risk response plan is not initiated through a formal project change management procedure. Risk response is part of the project management plan and does not require a formal change control process because it has already been approved as part of the risk management plan. Alternatively, some organizations strictly follow a formal process for any change, specifically where there is dependency with a customer and joint development is happening.

7.2.6 Monitoring Project Risk

Monitoring risks at the project level consists of:

- Checking the status of the risks that have already been identified,

- Verifying whether any known risk has not occurred or is not about to occur,

- Monitoring the status of all actions implemented to respond to the detection or occurrence of a risk,

- Monitoring the remaining contingency reserve and management reserve,

- Observing the risk trends and profile,

- Assessing the project's key performance indicators and key risk indicators, and

- Ensuring effective communication among the team members and stakeholders, particularly the risk owners and risk response owners.

Capturing newly identified risks is imperative, as it helps ensure effective monitoring of project risks. This process involves promptly identifying emergent risks to address them effectively. These activities typically lead to updates of plans, registers, and controlling documents. In addition, performance reports are regularly analyzed to identify any potential trends that could indicate new risks or the ineffectiveness of response strategies.

The risk responses implemented to anticipate and prevent the occurrence of threats or exploit and enhance opportunities are conducted according to their quantitative parameters of time, cost, scope, and specifications. A qualitative assessment evaluates the effectiveness and efficiency of risk treatment for specific risks that have occurred.

Case Study: Monitoring Project Risk in the Compact Wind Turbine Project

Referring to the Compact Wind Turbine Project, the project manager and project team conduct regular risk revisits. The status of inherent and secondary risks, risk ratings, treatment actions, and their efficiency and effectiveness are monitored. Project management plans, documents, and registers are updated. Reports are generated and distributed to internal stakeholders within the municipality. Systemic risks are also reported to the portfolio level and senior management for high-level analysis and actions.

7.3 Integration of Risk Management into Project Management Processes

The subsequent sections offer detailed insights into integrating risk processes across the project life cycle. *Process Groups: A Practice Guide* [7] outlines the Project Management Process Groups and risk management processes. While Process Groups are conventionally associated with predictive approaches, this practice guide ensures inclusivity by addressing adaptive and hybrid approaches.

7.3.1 Initiating Processes

Initiating processes are performed to define a new project or a new phase of an existing project by obtaining authorization to start the project or phase. An essential part of that work is related to understanding the high-level risks that may impact the realization of objectives specified in the business case. It is essential to address these risks before authorizing the project or phase.

Another important consideration is the selection of the project management life cycle early in the project initiation. As summarized in Section 4, adaptive, predictive, and hybrid project management life cycles are varied based on flexibility, transparency, frequent delivery, and feedback in risk management. Utilizing each one of them has an impact on all areas of project management risk identification. The structure of the risk management, communications, risk monitoring, and feedback can exploit opportunities or introduce new threats to the project.

Another important aspect is understanding the risks related to the key stakeholders, their interests, and potential conflicts during the project initiations. Unresolved stakeholder conflicts can have negative implications for both the realization of project benefits and the acceptance of project deliverables, thereby impacting the overall success and effectiveness of the project.

In addition, implementing a "premortem" during project initiation can help identify future events that may hinder project objectives and uncover factors that can enhance success. Anticipating failure scenarios and assessing resource utilization allows for early risk identification and brainstorming response strategies, thereby increasing project success chances.

7.3.2 Planning Processes

Planning processes establish the scope of the project, refine the objectives, and define the course of action required to attain the objectives that the project was undertaken to achieve.

The selection of the overall risk management approach is one of the key planning decisions. This decision involves the analysis of risks that could potentially impact the effectiveness of the risk management processes.

The key areas of planning that also include risk management practices are:

- Integrity of the planning processes and the resulting plans, and

- Selection of the management approaches in all areas relevant to the project as well as estimation activities.

Typically, initiating processes lead to the identification of a high number of risks because they include analytical work necessary for planning. During this planning phase, more information is revealed about the agreed-upon timeframes, contingencies, methods of delivery, constructability, and procurements. It is important to ensure that risk identification becomes a natural part of every process.

7.3.3 Executing Processes

Executing processes are performed to complete the work defined in the project management plan to satisfy requirements and achieve objectives. Successful risk management depends on the flow of knowledge within the project and the organizations involved in its execution.

Risk management practices are most effective when supported by a culture that embraces proactive behavior, open communication, organizational learning, continuous improvement, innovation, and the use of tools such as big data and artificial intelligence. Integration of risk management practices with team building and management, transparency, quality management, habits of testing and learning, execution of stakeholder engagement strategies, and communication processes is essential.

7.3.4 Monitoring and Controlling Processes

Monitoring and Controlling processes review and regulate the progress and performance of the project, identify the required preventive and corrective actions, and initiate the corresponding changes to bring the project back on track.

Risk management ensures the integrity and reliability of reporting on the project performance and is based on the key performance indicators (KPIs). Risk management life cycle processes utilize the performance data and information as key inputs to identify, analyze, plan responses, and monitor the risks of the project.

7.3.5 Closing Processes

Closing processes are performed to formally complete or close the project or phase. Risk management activities during project closure include documenting lessons learned to be shared with future projects and other functions within the organization. The useful information documented may include the risk breakdown structure, controls and treatment actions for specific project types, effectiveness of specific risk responses, and systemic risks and issues requiring escalation to higher management levels.

The remaining risks that could impact benefits realization are documented in separate risk registers and handed over to the operations team before project closure.

Case Study: Integration of Risk Management into the Project Management Processes in the Compact Wind Turbine Project

Initiating Processes

In the Compact Wind Turbine Project case study, the key stakeholder groups include the municipality, the energy management department, local community members, environmental sustainability advocates, media representatives, the project manager, material suppliers, subcontracting agencies, and agricultural landowners.

The project manager performs stakeholder analysis to understand their interests and impacts on the project objectives early in the initiation phase. They identify a conflict of interest between the property group and the agricultural landowners. The property group tends to negotiate the land easement based on experience and as per the allowed contingencies in the project budget. However, the inquiries from agricultural landowners reveal that they requested much higher amounts. Furthermore, when writing the business case, the project manager includes the risk in the project risk register with a set of high-level controls.

Planning Processes

In the planning phase, the project manager attempts to include a more realistic and accurate cost estimation for the land easements in order to prevent future corrective actions to the project budget or project scope. Based on the fact that more information is provided during the option engineering and concept design, the project manager consults the property group for more accurate prices of the agricultural lands in the area. As a result, more robust and accurate estimations can be included in the project contingencies.

Executing Processes

The project manager of the Compact Wind Turbine Project oversees the management of risks in the execution phase. Regular visits to the project risk registers, executing the risk response strategies and controls, and implementing the agreed-upon risk treatments should any risks materialize are among the actions in this phase. The contingencies are released into the project budget for implementing the risk treatments. Furthermore, residual risks are assessed and planned during project execution.

For example, a risk of noncompliance with environmental regulations materializes as the result of delays to the wind turbine project schedule. There are some recent changes to the environmental standards and the compliance requirements have been updated for this type of project. The project team identifies purchasing a temporary license as the treatment action. The project manager revisits the risk after the treatment to ensure the risk of noncompliance is under control.

Monitoring and Controlling Processes

The project manager monitors the project performance based on the data and information collected regularly. The project manager monitors the effectiveness and efficiency of the risk responses, overall project risk profile, and treatment actions. The project team looks for trends in the overall project performance and communicates them to the internal and external stakeholders. Potential preventive/corrective actions can be undertaken by raising change requests to bring the project back on track and improve project progress.

Closing Processes

In the closing phase, the risk management lessons learned are documented to feed into the municipality's project management office (P MO) documents for future use. These documents include details of what went right and what went wrong when managing the Compact Wind Turbine Project. The effectiveness and efficiency of the risk responses and the residual risk ratings during the periodic reviews are shared with the wider stakeholders in the municipality. The feedback and level of stakeholder engagement in risk management efforts and trends are shared. In addition, a review of the overall project's risk management approach is conducted to identify improvements.

7.4 Project Risk Management Controls

The purpose of risk management within projects is to secure the optimal delivery of the unique product, service, or result for which the project was undertaken. Risk management controls help to achieve optimal delivery by seamlessly integrating risk practices into the project management life cycle. This approach ensures that risk management becomes a natural part of project management.

The selection, tailoring, implementation, and monitoring of particular controls in a given project are a part of the governance activities. In all cases where the term *risk* is used, both residual and secondary risks should be considered when appropriate.

References

[1] Project Management Institute (PMI). (2023). *PMI Pulse of the Profession®—Power Skills: Redefining Project Success*. PMI.

[2] Project Management Institute (PMI). (2021). *A Guide to the Project Management Body of Knowledge (PMBOK® Guide)*—Seventh Edition. PMI.

[3] Project Management Institute (PMI). (2017). *The Standard for Portfolio Management*—Fourth Edition. PMI.

[4] Project Management Institute (PMI). (2024). *The Standard for Program Management*—Fifth Edition. PMI.

[5] Project Management Institute (PMI). (2014). *Navigating Complexity: A Practice Guide*. PMI.

[6] Ambler, S. W., & Lines, M. (2022). *Choose Your WoW! A Disciplined Agile Approach to Optimizing Your Way of Working*. Project Management Institute (PMI).

[7] Project Management Institute (PMI). (2022). *Process Groups: A Practice Guide*. PMI.

Appendix X1
Contributors and Reviewers of
Risk Management in Portfolios, Programs, and Projects: A Practice Guide

The Project Management Institute is grateful to all of the contributors for their support and acknowledges their outstanding contributions to the project management profession.

X1.1 Contributors

The following list of contributors had input into shaping the content of this practice guide. Individuals listed in bold served on the Development Team and individuals listed in italics served on the Review Team. Inclusion of an individual's name in this list does not represent their approval or endorsement of the final content in all its parts.

Yasir Masood, PMI-RMP, PMP, co-lead

Jen Pavlov, CICA, PMI-RMP, PMP, co-lead

Hanan Awaad-Mohamed, DBA, PMI-RMP, PMP

Joe Campa, PMI-CP, PMI-RMP, PMP

Shirin Ebrahimi, MSc, PMI-RMP, PMP

Rosaline Liezel Ronell Hendricks, PMP

Kevin James Poe, BS, MS, MBA

Erick Sican, PMI-ACP, PMI-RMP, PMP

Kiron D. Bondale, DAC, PMI-RMP, PMP

Madelie Gerber, CCDM, PMP-PBA, PMP

Tong (James) Liu, PhD, ASEP, PMP

Syed Ahsan Mustaqeem, PE, PMP

Manisha Nigam, MLS, SAFe 6, PMP

Anup Seshadri, PMI-RMP, PMP, PgMP

Ramani Viswanathan, PMP

Abu Eyo Abu

Bola Adesope, CBAP, CSM, PMP

Masoud Aghajani, PhD, PMP

Sharaf Alattas, PMI-RMP, PMP

Abbas Alimorad, MA, MPEd, PMP

Akram Aljaadi, PMI-RMP, PMP, PfMP

Riyad AlMallak, PMI-RMP, PMP, PfMP

Hanan AlMaziad, PMP, PgMP, PfMP

Abdallah AlMousa

Alfredo Armijos, PMI-ACP, PMI-RMP, PMP

Sivaram Athmakuri, PMI-ACP, PMI-PBA, PMP

Om Prakash Bajpai

Smitha Balakrishnan, PSM, PSPO, LSSBB

Ellie Braham, ATP, RIMS-CRMP, PMP

Ralf Braune, PhD, PMP

Feren Calderwood

Santiago Cartagena, DASSM, PMP

Panos Chatzipanos, PhD, D.WRE, Dr Eur Ing

Nguyen Si Trieu Chau, PMP, PgMP, PfMP

Kristi Cummings, CBAP, PMP

G. Murat Dengiz, PMP

Nivita Dhameja

Gaurav Dhooper, PAL-I, CSAPM, PMI-ACP

Louisa Dixon

Sylvie Edwards

Jakub Ejma-Multanski

Awab Elameer, PMI-RMP, PMI-SP, PMP

Lucie Ellis

Amr Fayez, SFC, SSYB, PMP

Maria Ângela de Souza Fernandes, Eng., PhD, PMP

Glenn Fernandez, PhD, CIA, CBCI

Rui Luiz Barbosa Filho, MSc, DASM, PMP

Carlos Augusto Freitas, CAPM, DAC, PMP

Mark Gabel, PE, CVS

Amy Bretherick Gangl, MBA, CBAP, PMP

Jorge Palomino Garcia, Eng., MBA, PMP

Jorge Valdés Garciatorres

Theofanis Giotis, MSc, DAC, PMP

Aparna Grandhi, PMP

Kenyi Mitsuta Grillet, MBA, PMI-RMP, PMP

Jorge Lamadrid Guerrero, SITES AP, PMI-PBA, PMP

Kazuro Haga, PMI-RMP, PMP

Harry Hall, PMI-RMP, PMP

Jeff A. Harris, PMP

Eckhard Hauenherm, DPhil

Diego A. Hernandez

David Hillson, PhD, HonFAPM, PMI Fellow

Richard Hughes, PhD

Andrea Innocenti, Agile Hybrid Project Pro, CGEIT, PMP

Stijn Janssens

Val Jonas

Harikuttan K

Kamal Raj K

Rami Kaibni, CBAP, PMP, PgMP

James Kemp, PMP

Ahmad Khairiri, FIMechE, FIMM, FMySET

Konstantinos Kirytopoulos, PhD, Dipl. Eng., PMP

Henry Kondo, PMP, PgMP, PfMP

Arturas Kuliesas

Norat Kumawat

Abhilash Kuzhikat, Prosci, PMI-ACP, PMP

Chia Kuang Lee, CQRM, P.Tech, PMP

Daniel Alfredo Zamudio López

Sergio Oswaldo Lugo, MBA, CDBA, PMP

Rich Maltzman, PMP

Haryanni Binti Masarip, GPM-b, PMI-ACP, PMP

Brian McCarthy

Smita Mishra

Subrat Kumar Mishra, PMI-RMP, PMP

Walla S.E. Mohamed, PMP, PgMP, PfMP

Azam Mohammed, PMI-ACP, PMP

Asaya Nakasone, PMP

Asad Naveed, PMI-RMP, PMP

Laurentiu Neamtu, PRINCE2, CSM, PMP

Laura Lazzerini Neuwirth, Agile Hybrid Project Pro, PMO-CP, PMP

Eng. José Ocando, PMP

Jason Orloske

Marcos Orozco-M, PhD

Yoshihisa Ozaki, PMP, PgMP, PfMP

David Augusto Borja Padilla, PMI-ACP, PMI-RMP, PMP

B K Subramanya Prasad, CSM, PMP

Zulfiqar Ali Qaimkhani, PMI-RMP, PMP, PfMP

Mohammed Abdul Rahim, DASSM, PMP

Hossein Rahmatjou

P. Ravikumar, PMP, PgMP, PfMP

Syed Ali Raza, PMI-RMP, PMP

Rafael Diaz Real, PhD, PMI-RMP, PMP

Alex Rebo

Pallav Rohatgi

Sergio Rojas A. Eng, MBA, PMP

Omar Samaniego, NEC, PMI-RMP, PMP

P. Seshan, PMI-ACP, PMI-RMP, PMP

Jeffrey Simoneau, PMP

Carlos Singh, PMI-RMP, PMP, PgMP

Tian Siqi

Lam Boon Soon

Mauro Sotille, MBA, PMI-RMP, PMP

Langes Supramaniam, MSc, BEng, PMP

Tetsuya Tani, CBAP, PMP

Frank Tank

Awadalsaid Tara

Shayne R. Taylor

Tom Van Medegael, PMI-ACP, PMP

Te Wu, PMP, PgMP, PfMP

Hany Zahran

X1.2 PMI Team Members

Special mention is due to the following PMI team members:

Warren Duffie

Julie Hardison, PMP

Tzarmallah Haynes-Joseph, MSc

Christie McDevitt, APR

Josh Parrott, MBI

Kim Shinners

Kristin Hodgson, MSML, CAE, CSPO

Appendix X2
Techniques for the
Risk Management Framework

Many techniques are in widespread use to support risk management processes. This appendix provides examples and highlights some of the most common and effective techniques that support the risk management life cycle. This information is not intended to explain the techniques in detail, but to list their most important characteristics. Those who are interested in learning more are encouraged to seek additional sources of information. Further guidance on the application of risk management in portfolios, programs, and projects can be found at PMIstandards+®, a dynamic platform that is a companion to PMI content. Use the QR code below to find more related subject matter. PMI membership or a subscription is required.

There are three major types of techniques: templates and lists, process techniques, and quantitative techniques. Templates and lists are designed to reflect industry and internal benchmarks and best practices as well as lessons learned. Process techniques make it easier to manage the risk management process and range from basic documents and spreadsheets to automated processes. Quantitative techniques support the analytical aspect of considering options and consequences in definitive terms.

The following sections describe some of the more popular techniques for each stage of the risk management framework. This list is not exhaustive, and several techniques are useful for more than one stage. Section X2.8 maps techniques to risk management stages where they may be useful. Some techniques are useful for more than one stage.

X2.1 Risk Management Planning

Plan Risk Management defines the approach to be followed for managing risks throughout the life cycle of the corresponding portfolio, program, or project. Planning sessions are recommended in order to build a common understanding of the risk approach among stakeholders and to gain agreement on the techniques to be used for managing risk. The risk management planning phase is usually supported by templates. The results of risk management planning are documented in the risk management plan. An overview of the key areas of focus is provided in Figure X2-1.

People	Tools	Business
Attitudes	Toolbox	Constraints
Roles, responsibilities, authority	Parameters	Amount of detail and effort
Communications	Definitions	Organizational agility

Figure X2-1. Key Areas of Focus for Plan Risk Management

Depending upon the size and complexity of the work, some or all of the following elements are present in a risk management plan:

- Introduction;

- Portfolio, program, or project description;

- Risk management methodology;

- Risk management organization;

- Roles, responsibilities, and authority;

- Stakeholder risk appetite;

- Criteria for success;

- Risk management techniques and guidelines for use;

- Thresholds and corresponding definitions;

- Templates;

- Methods for communicating risks to stakeholders;

- Strategy; and

- Risk breakdown structure.

There are several software tools available to assist with risk management planning. While not discussed here, many of the techniques listed in the following sections are incorporated in risk management software.

X2.2 Identify Risks

Risk identification is carried out in order to develop a comprehensive list of all known uncertainties that could have an effect on the portfolio, program, or project. All risk identification techniques have strengths and weaknesses. Best practices suggest using more than one technique to identify risks to compensate for any one technique's shortcomings and to increase risk identification rates. The main assumption in identifying risks is that biases and an array of human behavior patterns stand in the way of identifying unknown risks, identifying the wrong risks, or emphasizing or prioritizing the wrong risks. Some risk identification techniques are more helpful in identifying threats than opportunities or vice versa. It is important to balance the techniques used to target both threats and opportunities.

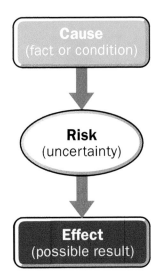

Figure X2-2. The Relationship among Cause, Risk, and Effect

Whichever risk identification techniques are used, it is important that identified risks are unambiguously described in order to ensure that the risk process is focused on the actual risks and not distracted or diluted by nonrisks. Use of structured risk descriptions can ensure clarity. Risk metalanguage offers a useful way of distinguishing a risk from its cause(s) and effect(s) by describing each risk using a three-part statement in the following form: "As a result of *cause*, risk may occur, which would lead to *effect*." The relationship among cause, risk, and effect is shown in Figure X2-2.

Risks can be identified based on checklists and templates, individual assessments, group risk assessments, external risk identification, etc. Individual assessments are performed by a single individual, whether an expert, stakeholder, or other participant. Individual risk assessments can be combined to create the overall risk register. Outside risk assessments can be generated by the enterprise risk management (ERM) function within the organization or provided by an outside source, such as a customer or supplier.

Sections X2.2.1 through X2.2.14 describe some of the common techniques for risk identification.

X2.2.1 Assumptions and Constraints Analysis

Assumptions are used to determine risk impact. They are statements accepted as true but need to be validated and continually reviewed during the iteration process and throughout the risk management work related to portfolio, program, and project life cycles. This technique requires three steps: (1) list; (2) test the validity; and (3) identify impacts on the portfolio, program, or project. An example is shown in Figure X2-3.

Another way of approaching assumption and constraint analysis is to use the following logic sequence:

- List the assumption or constraint.
- Test the assumption or constraint by asking two questions:
  - o Could the assumption/constraint be false?
  - o If it were false, would one or more objectives be affected (positively or negatively)?
- Where both questions are answered "yes," generate a risk, for example, in the form: *<Assumption/constraint>* may prove false, leading to *<effect on objective(s)>*.

Assumption or constraint	Could this assumption/constraint prove false? (Y/N)	If false, would it affect project? (Y/N)	Convert to a risk? (Y/N)

Figure X2-3. Example of a Constraint Analysis with Fields for Description and Analysis Results

X2.2.2 Brainstorming

Brainstorming is a technique for generating spontaneous ideas either individually or from a group of people. When brainstorming is used as a group risk identification method, the ideas and thoughts of one individual serve to stimulate ideas in the other participants.

X2.2.3 Cause and Effect (Ishikawa) Diagrams

The cause and effect (Ishikawa) diagram, or fishbone diagram (see Figure X2-4), is used to display root causes of risks visually, allowing deeper understanding of the source and likelihood of potential problems. The content is organized into a branching diagram where the causes may themselves have multiple potential sources so that the overview on risk stimulates additional thinking. The cause and effect diagram is also used to identify quality-related problems.

X2.2.4 Checklists

Risk identification checklists can be developed based on historical information and knowledge that has been accumulated from previous, similar portfolios, programs, or projects and from

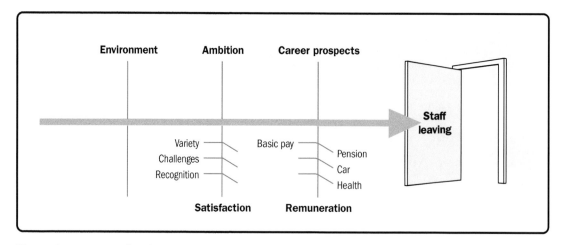

Figure X2-4. Example of a Cause and Effect or Ishikawa Diagram

Risk category	Subcategory	Example risks	Could this risk affect our project? Yes, No Don't know, Not applicable
1. Technical risk	1.1 Scope definition	Scope changes may arise during project.	
		Redundant scope may be discovered.	
		etc...	
	1.2 Technical interfaces	etc...	

Figure X2-5. Example (Partial) of a Checklist with Typical Structure of Category, Subcategory, Specific Risks, and Effect

other sources of information. The lowest level of a risk breakdown structure can also be used as a risk checklist. An example of a checklist is shown in Figure X2-5.

While a checklist can be quick and simple, it is impossible to build an exhaustive one. Care should be taken to explore items that do not appear on the checklist. The checklist should be reviewed during closure to improve it for future use.

X2.2.5 Delphi Technique

The Delphi technique uses a facilitated anonymous polling of subject matter experts to identify risks in their area of expertise. The facilitator gathers the experts' initial responses and circulates them without attribution to the entire group. The group members may then revise their contributions based on those of others. The process often generates a consensus of the experts after a few iterations.

X2.2.6 Document Review

A structured review of documentation may be performed, including plans; assumptions; prior portfolio, program, or project files; and other information. The quality of the plans, as well as consistency between those plans and the assumptions, can be indicators of risk.

X2.2.7 Expert Judgment

Expert judgment is the contribution provided to risk identification based on expertise in a subject area, industry segment, organizational processes, etc.

X2.2.8 Facilitation

Facilitation is the ability to effectively guide a group event to a successful decision, solution, or conclusion. A facilitator ensures that there is effective participation and that all contributions are considered.

X2.2.9 Historical Information

Historical records and data from past portfolios, programs, and projects help to identify common risks and prevent repeating mistakes.

X2.2.10 Interviews

Interviewing experienced portfolio, program, or project participants, stakeholders, and subject matter experts can identify risks. Interviews are one of the main sources of risk identification data gathering.

X2.2.11 Prompt Lists

Prompt lists enumerate risk categories with the purpose of detecting the risks that are most relevant to the portfolio, program, or project. A prompt list can be useful as a framework for brainstorming and interviews. Categories of risks include:

- Technical risks,
- Organizational risks, and
- External risks.

There are different types of prompt lists. Figure X2-6 provides examples of some of the better-known ones.

X2.2.12 Questionnaires

Questionnaire techniques encourage broad thinking to identify risks; however, questionnaires require quality questions to be effective.

PESTLE	TECOP	SPECTRUM
Political	Technical	Sociocultural
Economic	Environmental	Political
Social	Commercial	Economic
Technological	Operational	Competitive
Legal	Political	Technology
Environmental		Regulatory/legal
		Uncertainty/risk
		Market

Figure X2-6. Three Well-Known Examples of Prompt Lists That Can Be Useful for Risk Identification

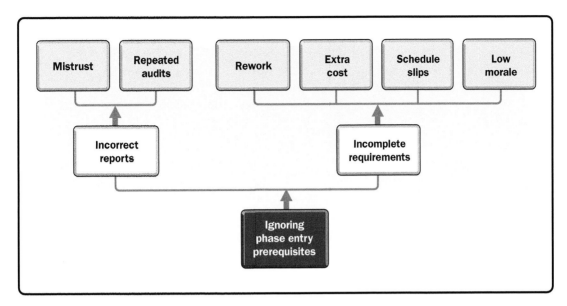

Figure X2-7. Example of a Root Cause Analysis

X2.2.13 Root Cause Analysis

Root cause analysis helps to identify additional, dependent risks. The identified risks may be related because of their common root causes. Root cause analysis can be the basis for development of preemptive and comprehensive responses and can serve to reduce apparent complexity. One way of diagramming root cause is shown in Figure X2-7.

X2.2.14 SWOT Analysis

SWOT (strengths, weaknesses, opportunities, threats) analysis is a technique that examines the initiative from each of the SWOT perspectives to increase the breadth of considered risks. It ensures equal focus on both threats and opportunities. This technique focuses on internal (organizational strengths and weaknesses) and external (opportunities and threats) factors. A method for structuring the results of a SWOT analysis is shown in Figure X2-8.

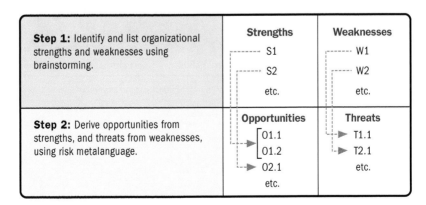

Figure X2-8. Example of a SWOT Analysis Structure

X2.2.15 Premortem

Premortem analysis is a strategic practice used to anticipate and address potential project failures. By envisioning the project's hypothetical failure and working backward to identify plausible causes, teams can proactively address risks before they materialize. This technique fosters a comprehensive consideration of vulnerabilities, enabling teams to devise preemptive measures for risk management.

X2.3 Qualitative Risk Analysis

Qualitative risk analysis prioritizes the undifferentiated list of risks that have been identified in the Identify Risks process for further evaluation or for handling. Organizations tend to apply resources to those designated as *high risk* based on their priority, often indicated by the risk's probability and impact characteristics. Qualitative risk analysis techniques are usually based on probability and impact but can also include additional prioritization variables. It is recommended to have a consistent, well-defined prioritization technique to maintain consistency among raters. An example of a rating definition schema is shown in Figure X2-9.

Sections X2.3.1 and X2.3.7 describe some common techniques for qualitative risk analysis.

X2.3.1 Affinity Diagrams

An affinity diagram is used to organize specific ideas or factors that contribute to a risk. It helps to sort risks by similarities or generic risk categories.

X2.3.2 Analytic Hierarchy Process

Analytic hierarchy process (AHP) is a matrix-method-based technique used to support a multicriteria decision-making process. It can also be used to identify risks. Even though there is an objective ranking where the subjectivity is minimized, the grouping is arbitrary. An example is shown in Figure X2-10.

Scale	Probability	± Impact on Project Objectives		
		Time	Cost	Quality
VHI	61–99%	>40 days	>US$200K	Very significant impact on overall functionality
HI	41–60%	21–40 days	US$101K–US$200K	Significant impact on overall functionality
MED	21–40%	11–20 days	US$51K–US$100K	Some impact in key functional areas
LO	11–20%	6–10 days	US$11K–US$50K	Minor impact on overall functionality
VLO	1–10%	1–5 days	US$1K–US$10K	Minor impact on secondary functions
NIL	<1%	No change	No change	No change in functionality

Figure X2-9. Example of Definitions for Levels of Probability and Impact on Three Specific Objectives Used to Evaluate Individual Risks

Preference Factors	
1	Equally preferred
2	Mildly preferred
3	Moderately preferred
4	Greatly preferred
5	Always preferred

Input Matrix (Preference Factors)				
	Cost	**Time**	**Scope**	**Quality**
Cost	1.00	0.25	0.33	0.20
Time	4.00	1.00	1.00	0.25
Scope	3.00	1.00	1.00	0.25
Quality	5.00	4.00	4.00	1.00

Note: Preference factors input into the shaded area of the matrix. Principal diagonal is 1.0 by definition.
Other cells calculated as 1/preference factor for same objectives.

Calculated Factors (Preference Factor/Column Total)					Weighting Factors
	Cost	**Time**	**Scope**	**Quality**	**Average of Row**
Cost	0.08	0.04	0.05	0.12	0.1
Time	0.31	0.16	0.16	0.15	0.2
Scope	0.23	0.16	0.16	0.15	0.2
Quality	0.38	0.64	0.63	0.59	0.6
Sum	13.00	6.25	6.33	1.70	1.0

Figure X2-10. Example of Analytic Hierarchy Process Computations to Determine the Relative Weighting of Four Objectives Related to a Project

X2.3.3 Influence Diagrams

An influence diagram is a diagrammatic representation of a situation showing the main entities, decision points, uncertainties, and outcomes, indicating the relationships (influences) among them. When combined with sensitivity analysis or Monte Carlo simulation, the influence diagram can identify risks to reveal their sources.

X2.3.4 Nominal Group Technique

The nominal group technique is an adaptation of brainstorming where participants share and discuss all issues before evaluation, with each participant participating equally in evaluation.

X2.3.5 Probability and Impact Matrixes

A probability and impact matrix allows the user to prioritize risks for further analysis or responses. It helps to distinguish between those risks that will have a minor impact on business activities and those that will have a major impact. It usually classifies risks according to their impact probability, such as very high, high, moderate, low, and very low. An example of a probability and impact matrix is shown in Figure X2-11.

X2.3.6 Risk Data Quality Analysis

Results of the risk analysis are only as good as the data collected. Review of the reliability and sufficiency of the data ensures that the analysis is based on high-quality information. Data that are deemed to be of lesser quality may be further researched or excluded from the risk analysis. Care should be taken when excluding poor-quality data to avoid a less-than-robust qualitative analysis.

X2.3.7 Assessment of Other Risk Parameters

Other characteristics of risk (in addition to probability and impact) can be considered when prioritizing risks for further analysis and action. These characteristics may include but are not limited to:

- **Urgency.** The period of time within which a response to a risk is to be implemented in order to be effective. A short period indicates high urgency.

- **Proximity.** The period of time before a risk may have an impact on one or more objectives. A short period indicates high proximity.

- **Detectability.** The ease with which the results of a risk occurring, or being about to occur, can be detected and recognized. When the risk occurrence can be detected easily, detectability is high.

- **Dormancy.** The period of time that may elapse after a risk has occurred before its impact is discovered. A short period indicates low dormancy.

Probability and Impact Risk Ranking											
Probability	**Threats**					**Opportunities**					**Probability**
VH	L	M	M	H	H	H	H	M	M	L	VH
H	L	L	M	H	H	H	H	M	L	L	H
M	L	L	M	H	H	H	H	M	L	L	M
L	L	L	L	M	H	H	M	L	L	L	L
VL	L	L	L	L	M	M	L	L	L	L	VL
	VL	L	M	H	VH	VH	H	M	L	VL	
	Impact (threats)					**Impact (opportunities)**					

Figure X2-11. Example of Probability and Impact Matrix Used to Sort Risks into Very High (VH), High (H), Moderate (M), Low (L), and Very Low (VL) Classes

- **Manageability.** The ease with which a risk owner (or owning organization) can manage the occurrence or impact of a risk. When management is easy, manageability is high.

- **Controllability.** The degree to which a risk owner (or owning organization) is able to control the risk's outcome. When the outcome can be controlled easily, controllability is high.

- **Connectivity.** The extent to which a risk is related to other individual risks. When a risk is connected to many other risks, connectivity is high.

- **Strategic impact.** The potential for a risk to have a positive or negative effect on the organization's strategic goals. When a risk has a major effect on strategic goals, strategic impact is high.

- **Stakeholder impact.** The degree to which a risk is perceived to matter by one or more stakeholders. When a risk is perceived as very significant, stakeholder impact is high.

X2.3.8 System Dynamics

System dynamics (SD) is a particular application of influence diagrams and can be used to further identify risks within a given situation. The SD model represents entities and information flows, and analysis of the model can reveal feedback and feed-forward loops that lead to uncertainty or instability. In addition, the results of an SD analysis can show the impact of risk events on overall results. Analyses of changes in the model or assumptions can indicate the system's sensitivity to specific events, some of which may be risks.

System dynamics exposes unexpected interrelationships among elements (feedback and feed-forward loops). It can generate counterintuitive perspectives not available through other techniques. The result is a view of the overall impact of all included risks.

X2.4 Quantitative Risk Analysis

Quantitative risk analysis is used to determine the overall risk to objectives when all risks potentially operate simultaneously. Techniques used appropriately for quantitative risk analysis have several characteristics: comprehensive risk representation, overall risk impact calculation, probability models, data-gathering capabilities, effective presentation of quantitative analysis results, and iteration capabilities. Quantitative risk analysis techniques enable representation of both opportunities and threats to the objectives.

Sections X2.4.1 through X2.4.7 describe some common techniques useful for quantitative risk analysis.

X2.4.1 Contingency Reserve Estimation

All of the conditional response plans, as well any of the residual risks will, if they occur, have an effect on objectives. An amount (time and cost) needs to be set aside to allow for these eventualities. This amount is made up of two components: (1) amounts to cover specific, approved conditional responses (e.g., contingency plans) and (2) amounts to address unspecified or passively accepted risks. Quantitative methods can be used to determine the amounts that should be set aside. These reserves are tracked and managed as part of the Monitor Risks process.

X2.4.2 Decision Tree Analysis

Decision tree analysis is used to determine partial and global probabilities of occurrence. It is a tree-like model that calculates the expected monetary value (see Section X2.4.4) of different possibilities by probability of occurrence. A simple example of a decision tree is shown in Figure X2-12.

X2.4.3 Estimating Techniques Applied to Probability and Impact

The probability of a risk occurring can be specified in several different ways. One common way is to assign levels of risk probability by ranges of probability. One benefit of this approach is that the subject matter experts only need to assess a risk's probability within a range rather than as a specific value.

Examples of impact-level definitions are very work specific. The values used to specify the level of impact from very low to very high (if a 5×5 matrix is being used) should be:

- Designated as higher impact for threats or opportunities as they move from very low to very high for a specific objective,

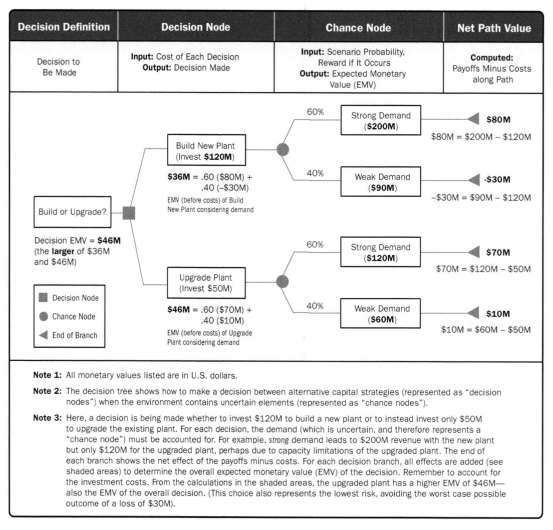

Figure X2-12. Example of a Decision Tree Diagram

- Defined by the organization as causing the same amount of pain or gain for each level across objectives, and

- Tailored or scaled by stakeholders to the specific work. The definitions, appropriately tailored, can be used for opportunities and threats.

If a risk's impact is uncertain and could be assigned to more than one level of impact (e.g., from moderate to high), the analyst may choose to assign the risk to the impact level that represents the expected or average impact. Alternatively, the risk may be flagged for extra analysis in order to reduce the range of uncertainty to fit within a single range.

X2.4.4 Expected Monetary Value

Expected monetary value (EMV) is a statistical technique that is used to quantify risks, which in turn assists the manager in calculating the contingency reserve. EMV is a calculation of a value, such as weighted average or expected cost or benefit, when the outcomes are uncertain. All reasonable alternative outcomes are identified. Their probabilities of occurring (summing to 100%) and their values are estimated. The EMV calculation is made for the entire event by weighting the individual possible outcomes by their probabilities of occurring. The formula is:

Expected monetary value (EMV) = Probability × Impact

X2.4.5 Failure Modes and Effects Analysis/Fault Tree Analysis

Failure modes and effects analysis (FMEA) or fault tree analysis uses a model structured to identify the various elements that can cause system failure by themselves, or in combination with others, based on the logic of the system. Fault tree analysis is often used in engineering contexts. It can be adapted for use to identify risks by analyzing how risk impacts may arise, or the probability of failure (or of reliability, mean time between failure, etc.) of the overall system, indicating the level of quality of the system or product. If the level of reliability is not acceptable, the fault tree can indicate where the system can be made more reliable; therefore, it is useful in the design and engineering phase of a program or project.

Failure modes and effects analysis assesses and analyzes the potential reliability of a system and/or products. It is used together with failure mode effect and criticality analysis as part of the general program to assess reliability of a system and potential failure modes.

Using historical data, the analysis of similar products/services, warranty data, customer data complaints, and any other information available may lead to the use of inferential statistics, mathematical modeling, simulations, concurrent engineering, and reliability engineering to identify and define possible failures.

Failure mode effect and criticality analysis (FMECA) is the logical extension of FMEA. It evaluates the criticality and probability of occurrence of the failure modes.

X2.4.6 Monte Carlo Simulation

Monte Carlo simulation is a technique to simulate probability distribution for a risk on an objective. The statistical method samples events to determine the average behavior of a system.

Monte Carlo simulation is a statistical analysis technique that can be applied in situations in which there are uncertain estimates, with the aim of reducing the level of uncertainty through a series

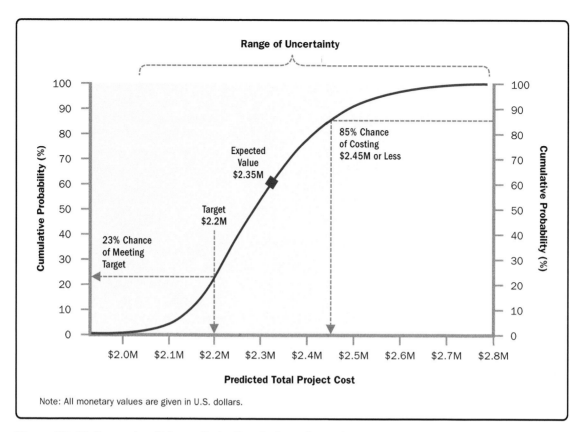

Figure X2-13. Example of Monte Carlo Simulation of a Project Cost

of simulations. In this sense, it can be applied in the analysis of risks associated with a particular objective. For each of the variables, Monte Carlo simulations do not provide a single estimate, but a range of possible estimates associated with each estimate and the level of probability that the estimate is accurate (confidence level) as shown in Figure X2-13.

X2.4.7 Program or Project Evaluation and Review Technique

Program or project evaluation and review technique (PERT) is a time-based technique that can be used to quantify risks at a given point in the development of a program or project.

X2.5 Plan Risk Responses

Plan Risk Responses develops the set of actions required to consider the risks and their characteristics and integrates them into corresponding plans and budgets. The resultant plan should satisfy the risk appetites and attitudes of the key stakeholders. There are three categories of techniques, as follows:

- Creativity techniques to identify potential responses,

- Decision-support techniques for determining the optimal potential response, and

- Implementation techniques designed to turn a risk response into action.

Respectively, these categories of techniques can be used to identify potential responses, select the most appropriate response to translate strategy into planning, and assign corresponding actions.

Identifying potential responses by a variety of creativity techniques is quite similar to risk identification techniques (see Section X2-2). Decision-support techniques assist in examining the trade-offs among risk response strategies. Such techniques also assist in choosing between preemptive prevention and contingency responses based on triggers.

Sections X2.5.1 through X2.5.5 describe a few decision-support techniques that may be used for the Plan Risk Response process.

X2.5.1 Contingency Planning

For specific (normally high-impact) risks, the risk owner may choose to assemble a team to develop a response as if the risk had genuinely happened. The corresponding plan, with the supporting information, is then documented and approved by management or the sponsor. This approval includes authorization to deploy the corresponding resources if the predefined trigger conditions arise.

X2.5.2 Force Field Analysis

Force field analysis is typically used in the change management context. It can be adapted for risk response planning by identifying driving forces (forces for change) and restraining forces (forces against change) that currently affect achievement of an objective. Risk responses can then be modeled based on the net result of the forces as shown in Figure X2-14.

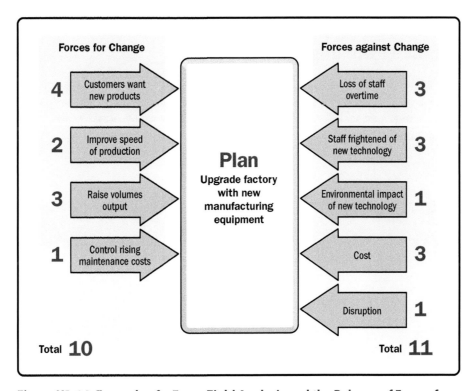

Figure X2-14. Example of a Force Field Analysis and the Balance of Forces for and against Change

X2.5.3 Multicriteria Selection Technique

Criteria for deciding whether to choose a specific risk response from among several options include cost, schedule, technical requirements, etc., as well as the risk attributes, such as the type of risk, magnitude of probability, and impact. Multicriteria selection could be weighted to reflect the importance of various criterion as shown in Figure X2-15.

X2.5.4 Scenario Analysis

Scenario analysis for risk response planning involves defining several plausible alternative scenarios. Each scenario may require different risk responses that can be described and evaluated for their cost and effectiveness. If the organization can choose among several scenarios, the alternatives, including responses, can be compared. If the scenarios are out of the control of the organization, the analysis can lead to effective and necessary contingency planning.

Scenarios usually include optimistic, most likely, and pessimistic assessments. The representation of optimistic and pessimistic scenarios can be useful in providing managers with a certain sensitivity to the upside and downside potential associated with a portfolio, program, or project.

X2.5.5 Simulation

Simulation is a technique to estimate the benefits and implications of different response plans versus the efforts and costs required to implement them. Simulations can also help analyze the possible implications to the critical chain in projects when implementing different risk response options.

X2.6 Response Plan Implementation

The most common technique to turn preventative response plans into action is adding them to the portfolio, program, or project management plan. While some planning techniques can keep track of and differentiate between tasks and actions that originated from response plans, some planning techniques will not differentiate between risk response tasks and other tasks.

Criterion	Weight	Option A		Option B	
		Rating	Points	Rating	Points
Price	9	8	72	10	90
Functionality	9	5	45	8	72
Ease of use	6	9	54	7	42
Lead time	7	9	63	6	42
Scores			234		246

Figure X2-15. Example of Multicriteria Weighting and Analysis

X2.7 Monitor Risks

Monitor Risks provides the assurance that risk responses are being applied, verifies whether they are effective, and as necessary, initiates corrective actions. Sections X2.7.1 through X2.7.10 describe techniques for monitoring risks during the entire portfolio, program, or project life cycle.

X2.7.1 Data Analytics

Data analytics supports the exploration of known risk types by analyzing related documentation and related data for applicability to a specific portfolio, program, or project. In direct data analytics, the question and types of risks explored are predefined, as are the relationships among different types of risks and their causes and effects. The use of big data, advanced analytics, or artificial intelligence capabilities to explore unknown types of risks are forms of advanced data analytics.

X2.7.2 Reserve Analysis

Reserve analysis is an analytical technique to determine the essential features and relationships of components in the work management plan to establish a reserve for the schedule duration, budget, estimated cost, or funds. Tracking the state of the reserve through execution provides summary information as to the evolution of the status of the corresponding risks. This information can be useful when reporting up through the organization's management structure. In addition, once a risk occurs or ceases to be current (i.e., when it can no longer impact), the corresponding reserve needs to be reviewed to assess whether it still provides the agreed-upon level of confidence.

X2.7.3 Residual Impact Analysis

Response plan implementation could lead to residual risks, emergent risks, or secondary risks.

X2.7.4 Risk Audit

Risk audits are carried out in order to evaluate the following:

- Risk management rules are being carried out as specified, and

- Risk management rules are adequate for controlling the work.

Section 7.4 introduces project risk management controls for project risk management governance. These project risk management controls then become criteria against which an audit is conducted.

X2.7.5 Risk Breakdown Structure

The risk breakdown structure (RBS) is a hierarchical framework of potential sources of risk. An organization may develop a generic or specific RBS. The RBS helps to identify specific risks in relation to its category and offers a framework for other risk identification techniques such as brainstorming. An RBS helps to ensure coverage of all types of risk and tests for blind spots or omissions. An example of a generic RBS for a project is shown in Figure X2-16.

RBS Level 0	RBS Level 1	RBS Level 2
All sources of project risk	1. Technical risk	1.1 Scope definition
		1.2 Requirements definition
		1.3 Estimates, assumptions, and constraints
		1.4 Technical processes
		1.5 Technology
		1.6 Technical interfaces
		etc.
	2. Management risk	2.1 Project management
		2.2 Program/portfolio management
		2.3 Operations management
		2.4 Organization
		2.5 Resourcing
		2.6 Communication
		etc.
	3. Commercial risk	3.1 Contractual terms and conditions
		3.2 Internal procurement
		3.3 Suppliers and vendors
		3.4 Subcontracts
		3.5 Client/customer stability
		3.6 Partnerships and joint ventures
		etc.
	4. External risk	4.1 Legislation
		4.2 Exchange rates
		4.3 Site/facilities
		4.4 Environmental/weather
		4.5 Competition
		4.6 Regulatory
		etc.

Figure X2-16. Example of a Generic Risk Breakdown Structure for a Project

X2.7.6 Risk Reassessment

Risk reassessment requires the following activities to be estimated and validated again to ensure effective control:

- Identifying new risks,

- Evaluating current risks,

- Evaluating the risk management processes, and

- Closing risks.

X2.7.7 Sensitivity Analysis

Sensitivity analysis is the evaluation of the effect on a variable by one or more influencing variables. Often used as a technique in monitoring risks, it serves to identify the possible impact on a given objective should one or more risks materialize.

X2.7.8 Status Meetings

Status meetings include the review of all open risks and trigger conditions that have occurred, leading to risks becoming issues. Risks responded to in the past period; effectiveness of the actions taken; impacts on the portfolio, program, or project; and lessons learned are formally recorded in a knowledge management system.

X2.7.9 Trend Analysis

Trend analysis evaluates how the risk profile changes over time, whether or not the previous actions resulted in the expected effect, and whether or not additional actions are required.

X2.7.10 Variance Analysis

The analysis of variances compares planned versus actual results. When the variances are increasing, there is increased uncertainty and risk. Outcomes from this analysis may forecast any potential for future deviation from the baseline plan prior to completion. Deviation from the baseline plan may indicate the potential impact of threats or opportunities.

X2.8 Risk Management Techniques Recap

Table X2-1 lists techniques for carrying out risk management in portfolios, programs, and projects. The list is not exhaustive, and it is not necessary to use all of the techniques.

The column headings list the risk management processes discussed in Section 4 of the practice guide and indicate a few of the strengths and weaknesses of each technique. Within each cell, the letters indicate a subjective evaluation of the relevance of each technique for the risk management process. In Table X2-1, the "C" stands for *core* and means that the use of that technique is recognized as useful in the context of a given process; the "S" stands for *supportive* and means that the technique can provide some useful information for a given process.

Table X2-1. Matrix of Risk Management Techniques Mapped to Risk Management Life Cycle Stages

Technique	Risk Identification	Qualitative Analysis	Quantitative Analysis	Response Planning	Risk Monitoring	Strengths	Weaknesses
Affinity diagrams		S		S		• Allows for grouping of ideas by common attributes	• May miss nuances of individual risks
Analytic hierarchy process		C	S			• Assists in developing a relative weighting for objectives that reflects the organization's priorities • Assists the creation of an overall priority list of risks created from the risks' priority levels with respect to individual objectives	• Organizational decisions are often made by committees, and individuals may not agree on the relative priority among objectives • Difficult to gather the information about pair-wise comparison of the objectives from high-level management
Assessment of other risk parameters		C		S	S	• Gives additional perspectives on risks • Helps to plan actions at the right time • Helps to identify additional needs for monitoring mechanisms	• Could make the qualitative analysis more complicated
Assumptions and constraints analysis	C	S			S	• Simple, structured approach • Can be based on assumptions and constraints already listed in the charter • Generates work-specific risks	• Implicit/hidden assumptions or constraints are often missed
Brainstorming	C			S		• Allows all participants to speak their minds and contribute to the discussion • Can involve all key stakeholders • Creative generation of ideas	• Requires attendance of key stakeholders at a workshop; therefore, can be expensive and difficult to arrange • Prone to groupthink and other group dynamics • May produce biased results if dominated by a strong person • Often not well facilitated • Generates nonrisks and duplicates; requires filtering
Cause and effect (Ishikawa) diagrams	C	S		S		• Visual representation; promotes structured thinking	• Diagram can quickly become overly complex
Checklists	C	S		S	S	• Captures previous experience • Presents detailed list of risks	• Checklist can grow to become unwieldy • Risks not on the list will be missed • Often only includes threats and misses opportunities
Contingency planning		S	S	C		• Ensures that actions are available to address significant events before their occurrence • Allows rapid and focused response • Improves image of professionalism of the way in which the work is managed	• Can give a false feeling of confidence—as if the risk has been avoided
Contingency reserve estimation			C	S	S	• Provides a rationale for reserves • Basis for constructive discussion with sponsor	• Makes the reserve visible and therefore liable to be reduced arbitrarily

Table X2-1. Matrix of Risk Management Techniques Mapped to Risk Management Life Cycle Stages (Continued)

Technique	Risk Identification	Qualitative Analysis	Quantitative Analysis	Response Planning	Risk Monitoring	Strengths	Weaknesses
Data analytics	S		S		C	• Enables complex analysis • Provides insights that might otherwise be missed	• Requires significant investment of resources to build • Relies on consistency of data input
Decision tree analysis		S	C	C		• Causes the organization to structure the costs and benefits of decisions when the results are determined in part by uncertainty and risk • Solution of the decision tree helps select the decision that provides the highest expected monetary value or expected utility to the organization	• Sometimes difficult to create the decision structure • Probabilities of occurrences can be difficult to quantify in the absence of historical data • The best decision may change with plausible changes in the input data, meaning that the answer may not be stable • The organization may not make decisions based on a linear expected monetary value basis, but rather on a nonlinear utility function; utility functions are difficult to specify • Decision tree analysis of complicated situations requires specialized software • There may be some resistance to using technical approaches to decision-making
Delphi technique	C	S		S		• Captures input from technical experts • Removes sources of bias	• Limited to technical risks • Dependent on actual expertise of experts • May take longer time than available due to iterations of the experts' inputs
Document review	C					• Exposes detailed risks • Requires no specialist tools	• Limited to risks contained in documentation
Estimating techniques applied to probability and impact		C	C	S		• Addresses both key dimensions of a risk, namely its degree of uncertainty (expressed as probability) and its effect on objectives (expressed as impact)	• Difficult to calibrate if there is no historical database of similar events • Terms for probability (e.g., probable, almost certain) and for impact (e.g., insignificant, major) are ambiguous and subjective • Impacts can be uncertain or represented by a range of values that cannot be put into a specific impact level such as "moderate impact on time"
Expected monetary value (EMV)			C			• EMV allows the user to calculate the weighted average (expected) value of an event that includes uncertain outcomes • Well suited to decision tree analysis • EMV incorporates both the probability and impact of the uncertain events • EMV is a simple calculation that does not require specialized software	• Assessment of probability of risk events occurring and of their impact can be difficult to make • EMV provides only the expected value of uncertain events; risk decisions often require more information than EMV can provide • EMV is sometimes used in situations where Monte Carlo simulation would be more appropriate and provide additional information about the risk
Expert judgment	C	C	S	S	S	• Provides experiential perspective • Multiple experts increase breadth and depth	• Can be subject to biases based on experience • Potential for limited perspective
Facilitation	C			S		• Enables broad participation and diverse perspectives	• Can be time-consuming • Subject to groupthink bias

(Continued)

Table X2-1. Matrix of Risk Management Techniques Mapped to Risk Management Life Cycle Stages *(Continued)*

Technique	Risk Identification	Qualitative Analysis	Quantitative Analysis	Response Planning	Risk Monitoring	Strengths	Weaknesses
Fault tree analysis (FMEA/ FMECA)	C		C	S		• Structured approach; well understood by engineers • Produces an estimate of overall reliability using quantitative tools • Good tool support	• Focuses on threats; not so useful for opportunities • Requires expert tools not generally available to others
Force field analysis	C	S		S		• Creates deep understanding of factors that affect objectives	• Time-consuming and complex technique • Usually only applied to a single objective, so does not provide whole view
Historical information	C	C	C	C	S	• Leverages previous experience • Prevents making the same mistakes or missing the same opportunities • Enhances the organizational process assets	• Limited to those risks that occurred previously • Information is frequently incomplete: lacks detail of past risks and may not include details of successful resolution; ineffective strategies are rarely documented
Influence diagrams	C	C		S		• Exposes key risk drivers • Can generate counterintuitive insights not available through other techniques	• Requires disciplined thinking • Not always easy to determine appropriate structure
Interviews	C				C	• Addresses risks in detail • Generates engagement of stakeholders	• Time-consuming • Raises nonrisks, concerns, issues, worries, etc.; therefore, requires filtering
Monte Carlo simulation			C	S		• Used primarily for project schedule and cost risk analysis in strategic decisions • Allows all specified risks to vary simultaneously • Calculates quantitative estimates of overall risk; reflects the reality that several risks may occur together • Provides answers to questions such as: (1) How likely is the base plan to be successful? (2) How much contingency in time and cost do we need to achieve our desired level of confidence? (3) Which activities are important in determining the overall risk?	• Schedules are not simple and often cannot be used in simulation without significant debugging by an expert scheduler • Quality of the input data depends heavily on the expert judgment and the effort and expertise of the risk analyst • Simulation is sometimes resisted by management as being unnecessary or too sophisticated compared to other, more traditional techniques • Monte Carlo simulation requires specialized software, which must be acquired and learned, causing a barrier to its use • Produces unrealistic results unless input data include both threats and opportunities
Multicriteria selection technique		S		C		• Provides a means of selecting the responses that best support the full set of objectives	• Can give counterintuitive results
Nominal group technique	S	C				• Encourages and allows all participants to contribute • Allows for different levels of competence in common language • Provides ideal base for affinity diagramming (grouping by risk categories for use in the risk breakdown structure and root cause analysis)	• Can lead to frustration in dominant members who feel it is moving slowly

Table X2-1. Matrix of Risk Management Techniques Mapped to Risk Management Life Cycle Stages (Continued)

Technique	Risk Identification	Qualitative Analysis	Quantitative Analysis	Response Planning	Risk Monitoring	Strengths	Weaknesses
Program or project evaluation and review technique (PERT)			C	S		• Provides a time-based view of risks • Useful for observing the degree to which a risk takes on greater significance at a given point in time	• Does not have a defined measure of impact
Probability and impact matrix		C		S	S	• Allows the organization to prioritize the risks for further analysis (e.g., quantitative) or risk response • Reflects the organization's level of risk threshold	• Does not explicitly handle other factors such as urgency or manageability that may partly determine a risk's ranking • Range of uncertainty in the assessment of a risk's probability or impact may overlap a boundary
Prompt lists	C			S		• Ensures coverage of all types of risk • Stimulates creativity	• Topics can be too abstract
Questionnaire	C	S				• Encourages broad thinking to identify risks	• Success depends on the quality of the questions • Limited to the topics covered by the questions • Can be a simple reformatting of a checklist
Reserve analysis		C	C	C	S	• Provides a means of tracking spending and releasing contingency amounts as risks expire; can be applied to schedule reserves in the same way • Gives early warning of the need to communicate with sponsor	• Could lead to unwarranted focus on cost dimension • Attention to overall measure of reserve depletion may hide detailed risks
Residual impact analysis	C			S	S	• Provides for further analysis of potential risks after initial treatment is applied	• May promote focusing on risks that do not have substantial impact potential
Risk audit	S				C	• Provides a formal assessment of the compliance with the approach specified in the risk management plan	• Can be disruptive and taken as too judgmental to the team
Risk breakdown structure	C	S	S	S	S	• Offers a framework for other risk identification techniques such as brainstorming • Ensures coverage of all types of risk • Tests for blind spots or omissions	• Can lead to complacency where the fact that the risk is recorded is deemed adequate risk management
Risk data quality assessment		C				• Promotes consideration of the validity of risk characteristics	• May be difficult to quantify the accuracy of the data
Risk reassessment				S	C	• Forces a review of the risks when it becomes necessary so that the risk register remains current	• Takes time and effort
Root cause analysis	C	S	S	C		• Allows identification of additional, dependent risks • Allows the organization to identify risks that may be related because of their common root causes • Basis for development of preemptive and comprehensive responses • Can serve to reduce apparent complexity	• Most risk management techniques are organized by individual risk; this structure is not conducive to identifying the root causes • Can oversimplify and hide the existence of other potential causes • There may be no valid strategy available for addressing the root cause once it has been identified

(Continued)

Table X2-1. Matrix of Risk Management Techniques Mapped to Risk Management Life Cycle Stages *(Continued)*

Technique	Risk Identification	Qualitative Analysis	Quantitative Analysis	Response Planning	Risk Monitoring	Strengths	Weaknesses
Scenario analysis	C	S	S	C		• Provides view of the potential effect of the relevant risk and the corresponding response strategy • Forces the participants to analyze the effect of any strategy • Helps to identify secondary risks	• Adds to the list of assumptions • Can be time-consuming
Sensitivity analysis			C	S	S	• Enables a structured approach to evaluating potential impact of risks	• Suggests that the results are absolute because they have been given a quantified measure
Simulations	S		C	S		• Allows for analysis of multiple forces around a given risk or set of risks	• Can be difficult to build a comprehensive model • Often expensive to implement
Status meeting	S				C	• Provides a means of verifying information about the status of risks (active, occurred, retired) and maintaining team understanding	• Can seem unnecessary to some participants
SWOT (strengths, weaknesses, opportunities, threats) analysis	C	S		S		• Ensures equal focus on both threats and opportunities • Offers a structured approach to identify threats and opportunities • Focus on internal (organizational strengths and weaknesses) and external (opportunities and threats) risks	• Focuses on internally generated risks arising from organizational strengths and weaknesses; excludes external risks • Tends to produce high-level, generic risks
System dynamics	C	C		S		• Exposes unexpected interrelations between elements (feedback and feed-forward loops) • Can generate counterintuitive insights not available through other techniques • Produces overall impacts of all included risks	• Requires specialized software and expertise to build models • Focuses on impacts, but difficult to include the concept of probability
Trend analysis	S				C	• Provides an indication of the effectiveness of earlier responses • Can provide trigger conditions for responses	• Requires understanding of significant versus nonsignificant variation
Variance analysis	S				C	• Allows comparison between forecast and actual risk impacts • Can provide trigger conditions for responses • Provides data for earned value analysis, which can be compared to quantitative risk analysis results	• Does not show relationship with earlier data • Values can be taken out of context

Appendix X3
Risk Classification

Potential risks can be classified into one of four quadrants based on the degree of available information, ambiguity, and variability. Organizations work to reduce the degree of unknown factors so they can be progressively converted to known-knowns or, at least, known-unknowns. This appendix details this concept, which was introduced in Section 3 of this standard.

- **Known-known.** A known-known is a fact, not a risk. These facts are typically identified as part of the requirements and scope. The entity working on the endeavor is aware of these facts, which are incorporated into the portfolio, program, or project scope.

- **Known-unknown.** A known-unknown is an identified risk. The entity working on the endeavor is aware of the uncertain event and the potential consequences. Known-unknown risks are identified and proactively managed.

- **Unknown-known.** An unknown-known is a hidden fact. Knowledge about the fact may exist; however, the entity may not be aware of it at the time of the endeavor. An example of an unknown-known is a hidden or ignored assumption. The identification, assessment, and development of a strong understanding of unknown-known risks occur over time. For complex and innovative activities, there is a high degree of guesswork in which risks can be identified, but with limited visibility. Unknown-knowns are typically addressed through progressive risk elaboration integrated with execution of the endeavor.

- **Unknown-unknown.** Unknown-unknown risks may be emergent risks that are essentially unknowable within the context of portfolio, program, and project management. That lack of knowledge makes any type of evaluation or exploration impossible. Unknown-unknowns can be managed through organizational resilience. Due to unpredictability, resilient organizations promote research, raise awareness, encourage teams to question the status quo, and increase the flow of information. These actions stretch the boundaries of influence and prepare organizations to better respond to and recover from such events.

Glossary

Inclusions and Exclusions

This glossary includes terms that are:

- Unique to risk management (e.g., risk appetite), and

- Not unique to risk management but used differently or with a narrower meaning in risk management than in general everyday use (e.g., threat, cause).

This glossary generally does not include:

- Application- or industry-area-specific terms, or

- Terms used in risk management that do not differ in any material way from everyday use (e.g., business).

Definitions

Many of the words defined in this glossary may have broader and, in some cases, different dictionary definitions to accommodate the context of risk management.

Assumption. A factor in the planning process considered to be true, real, or certain, without proof or demonstration.

Cause. Events or circumstances that currently exist or are certain to exist in the future, which might give rise to risks.

Component. A predetermined element of a portfolio, program, or project that is work related to the achievement of the strategic objectives of the portfolio, program, or project.

Constraint. A limiting factor that affects the execution of a portfolio, program, project, or process.

Contingency Plan. A document that describes actions to take if predetermined trigger conditions occur.

Contingency Reserve. Time or money allocated in the schedule or cost baseline for known risks with active response strategies. See also *management reserve*.

Emergent Risk. A risk that arises that could not have been identified earlier.

Enterprise Risk Management. An approach to managing risk that reflects the organization's culture, capability, and strategy to create and sustain value.

Identify Risks. The process of determining and documenting the risks that might affect the intended outcomes.

Impact. A measure of the effect of a risk on one or more objectives if it occurs.

Issue. A current condition or situation that may have an impact on one or more objectives. See also *opportunity*, *risk*, and *threat*.

Management Reserve. Time or money that management sets aside in addition to the schedule or cost baseline and releases for unforeseen work that is within the scope of the portfolio, program, or project. See also *contingency reserve*.

Opportunity. A risk that would have a positive effect on one or more portfolio, program, or project objectives. See also *issue*, *risk*, and *threat*.

Organizational Project Management. A framework in which portfolio, program, and project management are integrated with organizational enablers in order to achieve strategic objectives.

Overall Risk. The effect of uncertainty on the portfolio, program, or project as a whole.

Portfolio. Projects, programs, subsidiary portfolios, and operations managed as a group to achieve strategic objectives. See also *program* and *project*.

Portfolio Management. The centralized management of one or more portfolios to achieve strategic objectives. See also *program management* and *project management*.

Probability. A measure of how likely an individual risk is to occur.

Program. Related projects, subsidiary programs, and program activities managed in a coordinated manner to obtain benefits not available from managing them individually. See also *portfolio* and *project*.

Program Management. The application of knowledge, skills, and principles to a program to achieve the program objectives and to obtain benefits and control not available by managing program components individually. See also *portfolio management* and *project management*.

Project. A temporary endeavor undertaken to create a unique product, service, or result. See also *portfolio* and *program*.

Project Management. The application of knowledge, skills, tools, and techniques to project activities to meet the project requirements. See also *portfolio management* and *program management*.

Qualitative Risk Analysis. The consideration of a range of characteristics such as probability of occurrence, degree of impact on the objectives, manageability, timing of possible impacts, relationships with other risks, and common causes or effects.

Quantitative Risk Analysis. The combined effect of identified risks on the desired outcome.

Residual Risk. The risk that remains after risk responses have been implemented. See also *secondary risk*.

Response Strategy. A high-level approach to address an individual risk or overall risk, broken down into a set of risk actions.

Risk. An uncertain event or condition that, if it occurs, has a positive or negative effect on one or more portfolio, program, or project objectives. See also *issue, opportunity,* and *threat*.

Risk Acceptance. A risk response strategy that involves acknowledging the risk and taking no action unless it occurs. Acceptance of the risk's implication(s) usually means using schedule and/or cost reserves and accepting scope and/or quality reduction(s). See also *risk avoidance, risk enhancement, risk mitigation, risk sharing,* and *risk transference*.

Risk Analysis. The activities related to defining the characteristics of a risk and the degree to which it can impact objectives.

Risk Appetite. The degree of uncertainty an organization or individual is willing to accept in anticipation of a reward. See also *risk threshold*.

Risk Assessment. The process of identifying, analyzing, and determining the probability of occurrence of a risk and its impacts if it does occur.

Risk Attitude. A disposition toward uncertainty, adopted explicitly or implicitly by individuals and groups, driven by perception, and evidenced by observable behavior.

Risk Avoidance. A risk response strategy that involves eliminating the threat or protecting the portfolio, program, or project from its impact. See also *risk acceptance*, *risk enhancement*, *risk mitigation*, *risk sharing*, and *risk transference*.

Risk Enhancement. A risk response strategy that involves increasing the probability of occurrence or impact of an opportunity.

Risk Escalation. A risk response strategy that involves transferring the ownership of the risk to a relevant party in the organization because the risk is outside of scope or the team does not have sufficient authority to address it.

Risk Exposure. An aggregate measure of the potential impact of all risks at any given point in time in a portfolio, program, or project.

Risk Identification. The process of locating and profiling the characteristics of risks related to work objectives.

Risk Management. Activities used to identify, analyze, respond to, and monitor risks at the enterprise, portfolio, program, or project level.

Risk Management Framework. A structure that organizes the process and activities of managing risks in an iterative fashion.

Risk Management Life Cycle. A structured approach for undertaking a comprehensive view of risk throughout the enterprise, portfolio, program, and project domains.

Risk Management Plan. A component of the portfolio, program, or project management plan that describes how risk management activities will be structured and performed.

Risk Mitigation. A risk response strategy that involves decreasing the probability of occurrence or impact of a threat. See also *risk acceptance*, *risk avoidance*, *risk enhancement*, *risk sharing*, and *risk transference*.

Risk Owner. The person responsible for monitoring the risk and for selecting and implementing an appropriate risk response strategy.

Risk Register. A repository in which outputs of risk management processes are recorded.

Risk Response. An action, planned or implemented, to address particular threats and opportunities.

Risk Sharing. A risk response strategy that involves allocating ownership of an opportunity to a third party that is best able to capture the opportunity or absorb the impact of the threat. See also *risk acceptance*, *risk avoidance*, *risk enhancement*, *risk mitigation*, and *risk transference*.

Risk Threshold. The measure of acceptable variation around an objective that reflects the risk appetite of the organization and stakeholders. See also *risk appetite*.

Risk Transference. A risk response strategy that involves shifting the impact of a threat to a third party, together with ownership of the response. See also *risk acceptance, risk avoidance, risk enhancement, risk mitigation*, and *risk sharing*.

Secondary Risk. A risk that arises as a direct result of implementing a risk response. See also *residual risk*.

Stakeholder. An individual, group, or organization that may affect, be affected by, or perceive itself to be affected by a decision, activity, or outcome of a portfolio, program, or project.

Threat. A risk that would have a negative effect on one or more portfolio, program, or project objectives. See also *issue, opportunity*, and *risk*.

Trigger Condition. An event or situation that indicates that a risk is about to occur.

Index

Institutionalized process, in project
    management, 43
Integrated risk management, 66, 67, 79,
    99–101
Integration risks, 82, 84
Interdependency risks, 80, 82, 83
Interpersonal skills. *See* Soft skills
Interviews, 114, 130
Investment viability, 68
Ishikawa diagrams, 112, 128
Issue(s)
    definition of, 7, 9, 13, 135
    resolving, 13
Issue log, 9
Iterative approach to risk management, 36
Iterative qualitative risk analysis, 51
Iterative risk identification, 48

K

Key performance indicators (KPIs), 100
Known-known risk, 30, 133
Known-unknown risk, 30, 133

L

Life cycle. *See* Risk management life cycle
Lists. *See* Activity lists; Checklists; Prompt lists

M

Machine learning (ML)
    in portfolio risk management, 65, 66
    in risk management, 5
Manageability, of risks, 119
Managed process, in project management,
    43–44
Management reserve, definition of, 136
Market volatility, 68
Matryoshka metaphor, 38–39
Maturity levels of risk management,
    42–44
Minimum viable product (MVP), 27
Mitigation. *See* Risk mitigation
Monte Carlo simulation, 121–122, 130
Multicriteria selection technique, 124, 130

N

Nesting dolls metaphor, 38–39
Nominal group technique, 117, 130
Noncompliance risk, 101

O

OPAs. *See* Organizational process assets
Open evaluation, 8
Operational risks, 81, 93–94, 95
OPM. *See* Organizational project management
Opportunities
    as benefits, 13
    in case study, 55–56
    definition of, 1, 9, 136
    enhancing, 22
    example of, 7
    explicit identification of, 49
    responses to, 9, 31, 55–56
    strategic, 88
    in SWOT analysis, 9, 115
Opportunity management, 9
Optimized process, in project management,
    44
Organizational commitment, to risk
    management, 18, 19
Organizational context, 24
Organizational culture, embracing risk
    management, 5
Organizational framework, 22–24
Organizational inertia, 21
Organizational levels
    and decision-making, 13
    risk across, 21, 22
    and risk management, 13–17, 74–76
Organizational planning, and risk management,
    24
Organizational process assets (OPAs), 94, 96
Organizational project management (OPM)
    definition of, 136
    levels of, 24
    risk management integrated with, 18, 19
Organizational risk management, 12–13
    in case study, 42
    program risk management aligned with, 79
    project risk management integrated with,
        38–41
    risk escalation in, 41, 42
Organizational strategy
    aligning risk management with, 4
    in nesting dolls metaphor, 38, 39
    and organizational environment, 21, 23
    portfolio management and, 22
    risk appetite and, 10–11
    risk-efficient boundary and, 64–65

Risk(s) *(continued)*
    operational, 81, 93–94, 95
    overall. *See* Overall risk(s)
    parameters of, 118–119, 128
    portfolio. *See* Portfolio risk(s)
    positive. *See* Opportunities
    program. *See* Program risk(s)
    relationship among cause, effect, and, 111
    residual. *See* Residual risks
    responding to. *See* Risk response(s)
    and reward, 63–64
    secondary. *See* Secondary risks
    sources of, 7, 8, 75
    strategic, 67, 68, 75
    structural, 15
    tactical, 67
    uncontrollable, 77
    unknown-known, 30, 133
    unknown-unknown, 30, 133
Risk acceptance
    active, 30, 53, 54, 55, 56
    definition of, 136
    passive, 30, 53, 54, 55, 56
    as risk response, 30, 31, 53, 54, 55, 56
Risk analysis. *See also* Qualitative risk analysis;
    Quantitative risk analysis
    definition of, 136
    in portfolio risk management, 68–69
    in program risk management, 81–83
    in project risk management, 92–93, 96
Risk appetite, 10–11
    definition of, 10, 137
    governance and, 12
    and organizational strategy, 10–11
    and risk-efficient boundary, 64
    in risk management plan, 45
    and risk threshold, 12, 91
Risk assessment
    automatic, 65
    definition of, 137
    factors for, 29–30
    open evaluation, 8
    periodic, 60
    in program risk management, 16, 17
    in project risk management, 17
    reassessment, 126, 131
    risk baseline and, 78
    of risk parameters, 118–119, 128

    of seriousness of risk, 12
    SWOT analysis, 8, 115
Risk attitude, 9–10
    changing, 10
    consistent, 10
    definition of, 9, 137
Risk audits
    periodic, 60
    purpose of, 125
    results of, 61
    strengths and weaknesses of, 131
Risk avoidance
    definition of, 137
    as risk response, 30, 53, 54
Risk awareness, 62
Risk baseline, 78
Risk breakdown structure (RBS), 125–126, 131
Risk checklists, 112–113, 128
Risk culture, consistent, 40
Risk data quality analysis, 118, 131
Risk description, 78
Risk efficiency, 15, 63–65, 78, 79
Risk-efficient boundary, 64–65
Risk effort, tailoring, 18, 19, 79
Risk enhancement
    definition of, 137
    as risk response, 31, 55, 56
Risk escalation, 41
    in case study, 42
    definition of, 41, 137
    effective, 41
    at enterprise level, 41, 42
    paths of, 45, 46
    at portfolio level, 41, 42
    at program level, 41, 42
    at project level, 41, 42
    risk appetite and, 45
    as risk response, 30, 31, 53–54, 55–56
Risk exploitation, as risk response, 31, 55, 56
Risk exposure
    definition of, 137
    in portfolios, 64
Risk factor(s)
    balancing, in portfolio risk management, 16
    definition of, 16